the Tenacious Nurse Nichols

the TENACIOUS *Nurse Nichols*

An Unsung AFRICAN AMERICAN CIVIL WAR HERO

EILEEN YANOVIAK

LP

LYONS
PRESS

Essex, Connecticut

An imprint of The Globe Pequot Publishing Group, Inc.
64 South Main Street
Essex, CT 06426
www.globepequot.com

Distributed by NATIONAL BOOK NETWORK

British Library Cataloguing in Publication Information Available

Library of Congress Cataloging-in-Publication Data Available

ISBN 9781493053339 (cloth : alk. paper) | ISBN 9781493053346 (epub)

♾™ The paper used in this publication meets the minimum requirements of American National Standard for Information Sciences—Permanence of Paper for Printed Library Materials, ANSI/NISO Z39.48-1992.

This book is dedicated to the undocumented Black regimental laundresses, cooks, and nurses of the Civil War, most of whom never received proper acknowledgment for their crucial role in the Union victory.

To my daughters, Lorelai, a nurse who cares for the most vulnerable people in our community, and Claire, whose heart continually grows in compassion.

CONTENTS

INTRODUCTION

IN APRIL 2018, I BEGAN MY ROLE AS DIRECTOR OF THE CARNEGIE Center for Art and History (renamed the Cultural Arts Center in 2023), a branch of the Floyd County Public Library in New Albany, Indiana. The museum features two long-standing exhibitions on Black history in the region: *Ordinary People, Extraordinary Courage: Men and Women of the Underground Railroad* and *Remembered: The Life of Lucy Higgs Nichols*, the subject of this nonfiction book. These exhibitions present the foundational research on the experiences of enslaved and free Black people and their communities in nineteenth-century southern Indiana. During the nineteenth century, New Albany was a bustling Ohio River town situated at the border of a slave state (Kentucky) and a free state (Indiana)—the infamous Mason–Dixon Line. Lucy Higgs Nichols was a Civil War nurse who escaped enslavement in Tennessee, joined the Indiana 23rd Regiment as contraband of war, and eventually found freedom and independence in New Albany.

When I became director of this small library-museum, I was among several people who now held the responsibility of sharing Lucy's story with the general public. Her story is compelling, filled with bravery, devastation, grief, glory, and dignity. We can all learn a great deal from Lucy's trials and tribulations. Her narrative needs to be preserved and shared. I am grateful for the opportunity to compile the research into a book with the permission of those that did the bulk of the legwork. The story of researching, preserving, and sharing Lucy's legacy is covered in the epilogue to this book, and there are many people who should be recognized for their heroic and diligent efforts. This book would not exist without their primary source research.

In 2019, I presented Lucy's story at a conference—the impetus for this book. I was one of several panelists in a session focused on the Underground Railroad at the Association for the Study of African American Life and History. Out of the five or so panelists, there was not a single African American scholar in the session. Once we had all presented, the first comment from the audience pointed out this very obvious and egregious omission. How could a panel of white scholars presume to understand the experiences of enslaved African Americans seeking freedom? How could our presentations not veer into white savior narratives that disproportionately acknowledge the contributions of white people? The experience put into high contrast the challenges that lie ahead.

Soon after I committed to this writing project, the pandemic hit in March 2020, which revealed so many global inequities and heightened my awareness of the responsibility I now held. Swiftly on the heels of global shutdown, the killing of Breonna Taylor in Louisville, Kentucky, brought about a reckoning of racial injustice that reverberated around the world. As a resident of Louisville, right across the river from New Albany, where I worked, I felt the need to do something meaningful. And simultaneously, I felt powerless, apathetic, and disingenuous. So I spent that year learning and listening while the world finally decided that equity actually mattered—in our homes, our communities, our workplaces, everywhere. We confronted racism even if we did not solve it. We had difficult conversations about difficult histories. We were compelled to acknowledge our implicit biases and do better.

I have grappled with and sometimes been crippled by the knowledge that I am a highly educated white woman writing the story of an enslaved Black woman. And while I can relate to some of Lucy's very human struggles as a woman and mother, her generational trauma is not my own, and I cannot truly understand what tragedies and barriers she had to overcome because of her race and history. I also recognize that financially benefiting from the writing of a book about a Black woman perpetuates systematized inequality. Yet I still feel compelled and responsible for writing this book. Fiction author Ann Patchett once said that "the thought of losing all the souls inside [her] was unbearable." Her characters were her responsibility, and that is how I feel toward Lucy.

Therefore, I pledge to donate a portion of proceeds from this book to an organization that works to preserve local Black histories and supports emerging Black historians. This book is dedicated to the people whose voices have been erased by time and to those who persevere in preserving the past.

The enormity of history—slavery, the Civil War, Reconstruction, and the civil rights movement—are made tangible through the stories of individuals such as Lucy Higgs Nichols. Lucy's story is uniquely inspiring, but she is part of a much bigger narrative. Her tenacious struggle connects her to the long civil rights movement, whose foundation is a "continuum of resistance" from Africans and Black Americans throughout America's troubled history. Historians Cheryl Janifer LaRoche and Patsy Fletcher explain this continuum: "Civil rights implies justice under the law in the form of legal actions taken by the government to create equal conditions for all people, civil liberties refer to protections against government actions, equal rights refers to equality before the law, human rights are the rights held in common by all, and natural rights are thought to be beyond the authority of any government or international body to dismiss. In the face of denial or curtailment of their legal rights, infringement of their civil liberties, and deprival of equal rights, African Americans frequently circumvented convention or pushed beyond legal confines in the quest for fulfillment of their natural and human rights."

The title of this book was carefully chosen to acknowledge Lucy Higgs Nichols's contribution to the Civil War effort. Affectionately called "Aunt Lucy" by the troops, she was denied the respect of the official title of "Nurse" because of her race. Although she did not marry John Nichols until after the war, I chose to honor her chosen name in freedom—Nichols—rather than the name of her enslavers. Nurse Lucy Nichols broke through barriers of race, gender, personal grief, and unimaginable oppression. She navigated a fraught cultural and political post–Civil War landscape to build a life that honored her worth. Ultimately, this is Lucy's true legacy: her quest for natural and human rights.

1

HIGGS FAMILY PROPERTY

THERE ARE ONLY TWO KNOWN PHOTOGRAPHS OF LUCY HIGGS NICHOLS, a Black American woman who was born into bondage, escaped enslavement, joined the ranks of the Indiana 23rd Regiment in the Civil War as a nurse, and fought Congress for her veterans' pension. In one large black-and-white group photo from 1898, she stands resolute and dignified with a serious but kind expression. She is surrounded by several veterans of the Civil War more than thirty years after they mustered out. Her stately gown and dark skin distinguish her from her male counterparts. She is one of them and yet distinctly different. The photograph is powerfully symbolic of Lucy's life. In a country where slavery coexisted with the belief in "life, liberty, and the pursuit of happiness," Black men and women had to forge new paths toward equality. Lucy's quest—for freedom from enslavement and toward equal rights for Black women in Reconstruction America—forms the foundation of the modern civil rights movement. Her harrowing story is just one example of the many Black Americans whose acts of resistance guided a nation toward a more just future that guaranteed inalienable natural rights for all.

Lucy Higgs was born into bondage in 1838. By the time she was eight years old, she had moved between three different states and been

Civil War and Spanish-American War veterans' reunion, English, Indiana, 1898.
Courtesy of the Floyd County Library, New Albany, Indiana.

at the mercy of four different masters. Although the property of only one family over her twenty-four years of enslavement, her young life was marred by instability, as she was passed between heirs, separated from family members, and moved numerous times.

The only known facts of Lucy's early childhood are eked from the records of her enslavers, the Higgs family of North Carolina. Their family dynasty casts a shadow over Lucy's early life. Before Lucy was even born, in the early 1800s, Jacob (1768?–1822) and Sally Higgs (1772–after 1837) were influential members of their community. The Higgs family farm of about 625 acres—a massive farm for that time period—was in Halifax County, North Carolina, near Scotland Neck. Jacob and Sally had three daughters—Sally, Judith (Judea), and Mary—and four sons—Joseph, Jacob, Reuben and William (Willie). The 1810 census included ten enslaved people belonging to the Higgs household.

Much of what is known about the Higgs family is gleaned from court documents, such as Jacob Higgs's will and testament. In the early 1800s, the last will and testament of a man, especially one with significant holdings such as Jacob Higgs, reveals the familial hierarchy of white men and women as well as the fates of the people they enslaved. All the material, land, and human possessions belonged to the patriarch of the family. Jacob Higgs's will, signed on December 22, 1816, left his wife Sally two feather beds and other furniture, three horses, and provisions to support her and family for one year. He "lends" his wife, for her lifetime, the tract of land on which he lived and many household possessions, such as spinning wheels and kitchen appliances plus four "negroes": Jacob, Charles, Gary, and Harvey. Dower laws in the 1800s essentially guaranteed widows the immediate support they needed to survive but little or no independence or ownership to sell property. Therefore, the people enslaved by Jacob Higgs and listed among his possessions may only be lent to his wife. They would eventually become the possessions of his sons and daughters.

Jacob had already established a profitable lifestyle, and he wanted to ensure that his children, particularly the boys, benefited from his hard work. Slave ownership in North Carolina was highly desired by upwardly mobile white landowners seeking to develop a monoculture (or restricted crop) farmstead for the market. While costly by the 1800s, slave owning offset a labor shortage and was the path to economic wealth. To his son Joseph, Jacob gave 230 acres and $150 to complete his education. To his son Willie, he gave another tract of land on Deep Creek—a substantial 430 acres—on the condition that he paid his brother Joseph $300 on his twenty-first birthday.

In contrast, to his daughter Sally, he gave one enslaved woman named Siller[?] and her child Meranza plus her mother's slaves on her mother's death. To Judea, he promises sufficient funds to purchase her own female slave and $250 for her education. Families who owned slaves made calculated decisions in the distribution of wealth to their heirs, and that may have looked different at different points in the lives of their children. Slave-owning parents were reluctant to give land to their daughters and more frequently gave them slave property. The expectation was that girls would maintain control over those slaves. By the late eighteenth century, southern slaveholders also recognized the virtues of educating women to meet their responsibilities as republican mothers. Unlike their northern neighbors, southern families did not typically educate their daughters with the goal of careers, nor did schools develop as frequently. Education, however, must have been a priority for the family because Jacob Higgs leaves money for education only to his younger sons Jacob and Reuben. Ultimately, however, when Jacob died in 1822, he did leave both enslaved people and legacy money, or a fixed sum of cash, to his four sons, including Reuben, who was at the time only twelve years old.

Jacob's wife Sally also left a will dispersing of property she had inherited, namely, slaves and farm animals. In her 1837 will, she bequeathed to her son Joseph two slaves: a woman named Beaty and a woman named Winney. To Jacob, she gave two slaves, Austin and Charles, plus some farm animals. To her son Reuben, she gave Nancy, Preston, Delila, and Delila's children. One of these women may have been the mother of Lucy, the heroine of this story, who was born only a year after this will was written. She also gave Reuben one slave named Viney in a trust for her daughter Sally. By leaving the slave in Reuben's name, she ensured that Sally maintained functional ownership of Viney. The matriarch stipulated that the slave not be sold on behalf of paying any debts for her daughter's husband William Whitehead and that the slave go to her grandchildren on her daughter's death. This interesting stipulation points toward Sally Higgs's understanding of coverture laws. Without the stipulation, coverture doctrine decreed that, on marriage, a woman's property passed into the hands of her husband. All her real property (land, slaves, wealth, and so on) came under his control. While he could not sell it without her consent, he did maintain control over and benefit from her property. Coverture laws worked on the assumption that a family functioned best if the male head of a household controlled all of its assets. Sally Higgs's will ensured that Whitehead could not control the slave assets that she bequeathed, and he would not inherit them on her daughter's demise. She closes her will with a statement of compassion for an enslaved woman by the name of Sarah, stating, "It is my will and desire that my sons Joseph and Reuben take particular care of my negro woman Sarah and see that she does not suffer." In the wake of her husband's death around a decade prior, Sally had clearly established a caring relationship with one of the enslaved women in her care, highlighting the paradox of benevolent slaveholders.

It is in the shadow of the Jacob Higgs family legacy that Lucy was born enslaved to the Higgs family in Halifax County, North Carolina, on April 10, 1838. There are no surviving records to confirm who Lucy's parents were. It is possible that Lucy descended from one of the people enslaved by the Higgs family—someone named in the last will and testament of Sally Higgs. Or perhaps she was the daughter of a slave purchased many years later.

Because the names of her parents are unknown, it is not clear how she received the name Lucy. Although African American slaves did not usually hold traditional African naming ceremonies, they did follow African tradition of naming children after relatives, a way of honoring the deceased and connecting past to present. Female babies received the name of their grandmother more often than that of their mother. Lucy was a common name for enslaved Africans and their descendants because the African names Latsi, Lesa, Leshe, Lisa, Lulu, Lumusi, Luri, Lusa, Luce, and Lushinda were often shortened to Lucy. Colonial slaves and their descendants generally controlled the naming process, but short-form names were often used because they could more easily be connected to the African origins, and slaveholders generally abided by these choices.

While no evidence of Lucy's childhood experiences survives either, accounts of the lives of other enslaved children help paint a picture of what Lucy's life might have been like. Enslaved children grew up all too quickly—they were essentially children without a childhood. They experienced separation, hunger, terror, misery, and despair from a very young age despite many efforts by their parents to shield them. They witnessed violence and lived in a perpetual fear of being sold. The trauma of living a life in bondage is likened to living in a perpetual state of war, and the psychological ramifications could be as severe.

Although the parents of children born into bondage are equally devoted to the well-being of their children as their free, white counterparts, children of slaves did not often have the benefit of long-term stable relationships with their parents, immediate kin, or even the fabricated extended families of fellow bondspeople. Many traditional African cultures were matrilineal, and women could rely on the support of other women in the community. Enslaved women who bore children, however, did not have that emotional and physical support system, and men were routinely sold separately from their families. The threat of separation loomed omnipresent.

Lucy's mother probably worked throughout her pregnancy. In some cases, pregnant enslaved women were assigned lighter labor loads alongside older slaves and children. There are accounts, however, of women being forced to work through excruciating medical conditions with little regard for health or comfort. Miscarriages were a common occurrence, often brought on by the labor load. Birth, too, was fraught with risk in the nineteenth century, especially for enslaved mothers, who often relied on female relatives or friends to deliver their babies rather than doctors or midwives like their white counterparts. If the mother were a slave, her child would be born a slave, too, regardless of the conditions of the father's freedom. Lucy's mother may also have had to raise Lucy without a father because the men were so often sold separately from their families. Unlike African communities that relied on a community of support after childbirth and during child-rearing, enslaved people in smaller slaveholding households would have been more isolated with fewer options for help from their community.

In the North American slave system, where ownership of people went on in perpetuity, parents had to teach children how to be children *and* slaves simultaneously. Children of slaves also became a financial matter for their owners. Each successful reproduction was a "profitable part of plantation life," according to Andrew Flynn, a white owner of at least forty slaves in Mississippi. As such, many slaveholders even acknowledged the marital relationships of their slaves, believing that a "happy" union could also be a profitable one. Lucy's father may have been from another household, a union "abroad," which most enslavers discouraged. If they had a child from the union, the profit of childbirth went to the enslaver of the mother.

The particular experiences of enslaved people varied according to several factors, including the region of the South, the crop they cultivated, the size of the plantation or farm, the wealth and disposition of the owners, and the composition of the slave community. The only consistent thing was that enslaved people's lives were contingent on the lives of their white owners. How we understand Lucy's life is based on the documented experiences of other slaves for whom there is more evidence. Lucy's future as a child born enslaved meant that she would work for the family from a young age. She would have learned to call the adult and child members of the household "Master" and "Missus" as a form of deference and respect, even for infants. Lucy was also likely brought up playing with her enslaver's children. As they aged, the white children took on the role of master, and the enslaved were their servants.

At what age Lucy began working is unknown. As Booker T. Washington once stated, "From the time that I can remember anything, almost every day of my life has been occupied in some kind of labor." Enslaved children had virtually no legal rights. Laws regulating child labor were not yet in place when Lucy was a young girl, nor would the laws have necessarily applied to the enslaved population. Young enslaved people were forced to work in all types of weather and for long hours. Children were introduced to jobs at a young age and expected to perfect their performance as they grew. The risk was that as they perfected a task, they became more valuable and, thus, more likely to be sold for a profit and separated from family. The typical age for a child to be put to work varied according to the standards of the owners. Often, the readiness of a child to perform labor was based on the "fractional hand system," a scheme that was devised to determine when a person was of age, young or old, to work full-time. Very young or very old people would be classified as "quarter-hand" or "half-hand," where a fully able-bodied adult would be a "full hand." Their classification not only would determine how much they worked at what tasks but also may have influenced how much food they received. In some settings, children would be working as soon as they could walk, gathering sticks for firewood, for example. As children matured, they received more demanding jobs based on their gender. Many of the men learned marketable trades, such as blacksmithing, that would prove useful after emancipation. Most girls learned skills, such as spinning, that were considered women's work, and therefore they were relegated to domestic servitude post-emancipation because they did not usually learn trades. Lucy might have learned a wide range of skills in her youth, survival among them.

The only constant in Lucy's young life was change. The 1830s, 1840s, and 1850s were tumultuous times for the Higgs family, and Lucy's fate was bound to their misfortunes. Lucy was born legally the property of the Higgs family, as were her older brother Aaron and sister Angeline. At some point before 1839, Reuben Higgs, then twenty-nine years old, took ownership of one-year-old Lucy and her siblings. At the time, Reuben was married to Eliza, the first of his two wives, and they remained on the family property in Halifax County, North Carolina. Eliza and Reuben had one child named Wineford Amanda Higgs. Soon divorced, Eliza and Amanda moved to Mississippi. The circumstances of the divorce are unknown, but it was certainly uncommon and leaves plenty of room for speculation.

Reuben quickly married his second wife and first cousin Elizabeth Higgs, born in 1817, the daughter of Theophilus Higgs Sr. and Mary P. Brantley. They moved to Hardeman County, Bolivar, Tennessee, in 1839, taking Lucy, her siblings, and their other slaves with them. This was Lucy's first time moving away from home at around one year old. Reuben and Elizabeth had four children: Wiley, Marcus, Prudence, and Jacob. Lucy's fate would lie in the hands of Reuben's five children, including the estranged Wineford Amanda. The surviving wills and court disputes are the only evidence of Lucy's young life, a point where she had no control over what happened to her, her family, and her scarce belongings. Lucy will eventually, some six decades later, find herself in control of her own destiny when she navigates the legal system to contest the will of her late husband and wins.

Still beholden to the will of her enslavers as a child in the 1840s, a series of tragedies befell the Higgs family that would uproot Lucy's life. Reuben's first wife, Eliza, died in Mississippi, leaving their daughter Amanda orphaned and under the care of a guardian named Samuel G. Wheeless. In nineteenth-century America, there was no official system for placing orphaned children. Widows did not automatically assume the care of their own children. There were, generally, five possibilities. The first, open to all classes of citizens, was for children to be indentured to nonrelatives to learn a trade. The second option was for an institution to oversee the child, sometimes to foster and other times as indentured. Another option was for widows to defy or challenge court rulings to petition for guardianship of their own children. Adoption was another informal option, not sanctioned by courts but socially accepted. Finally, open mostly to middle- and upper-class citizens and the one that befell Wineford Amanda was to be placed with a guardian. A system derived from English common law, the court-appointed guardian may or may not be family and had complete legal control over where the child lived, how the inheritance was spent (or governed as in the case of human lives), and what education was offered. He would also assume control of the bonded people who were inherited by Wineford Amanda. In fact, most guardians were in the business of guardianship for personal financial gain.

Reuben Higgs's property on Gray's Creek near Bolivar, Tennessee. Photograph courtesy of Pamela Peters.

Elizabeth, Reuben's second wife, died in 1844, and their son Jacob died only five months later. In 1845, when Reuben died, his remaining living children were left under the guardianship of their widowed grandmother Mary (Brantley) Higgs and later, for many years, under the guardianship of their uncle John Higgs (b. ca. 1811; d. ca. 1855).

Reuben's will stipulated that the people he enslaved were to be divided among his children, including Wineford Amanda, who at that time was the ward of her guardian Samuel G. Wheeless. In an inventory prepared by Wheeless of Wineford Amanda's possessions in 1846–1847, Wineford Amanda owned "two negroes," including "one little girl Lucy." Even though Wineford Amanda was herself an orphan and living with a guardian, she inherited Lucy and her sibling Angeline. Lucy, at only eight years old, and Angeline, twelve years old, were transported from Tennessee to Yalobusha County, Mississippi. Wheeless, the guardian, was sent to Bolivar, Tennessee, to fetch Lucy and Angeline. As ward, he charged the account of Winford Amanda seventy-five cents per day, plus eleven months' interest, for a sum of $8.60 for the journey that lasted about ten days. The journey via train, possibly along the Illinois Central line through Memphis, Tennessee, and carriage over ten days must have been incredibly scary for the two young girls. They were leaving their family, community, and home as they knew it, traveling across states with a stranger to take on new roles under the ownership of a young girl. Records from former slaves such as Lulu Wilson recall being a young child assigned duties in the house away from her mother, washing, ironing, cleaning house, and milking cows to please her mistress. Meanwhile, she would cry for her mother.

Girls such as Wineford Amanda and her half-siblings in the Reuben family learned how to be mistresses, or slave owners, from a young age through an instructional process that spanned childhood. They learned different discipline and management techniques. Often, slaves would be given to young children as gifts on special occasions by their parents. They often bequeathed them in wills, as had been done in Lucy's case. Thus, owning people as property was equated with financial success from a young age. Children who owned slaves practically grew up with them and cultivated bonds that could be both controlling and loving.

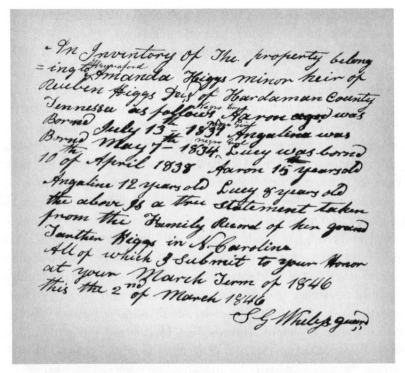

Inventory of property belonging to Wineford Amanda Higgs, 1846.

As a young girl owned by an orphan and overseen by a guardian, Lucy likely performed typical female duties. These might include but were certainly not limited to child care (though Amanda was a similar age) and housework, such as spinning, preparing and preserving food, cleaning, making and repairing clothes, and laundering. She probably also cared for poultry and livestock and made household items, such as soap and candles. Even if she was too young to cook, she may have helped prepare for meals doing many arduous tasks such as carrying water, picking and hauling vegetables, plucking poultry, and hauling wood and building fires. Given Lucy's skills as a nurse later in life, it seems possible that Lucy was trained to take on "house-girl" duties, an arguably prestigious position that required the enslaved person to exhibit a level of cleanliness, intelligence, and discipline that was becoming of a servant in the household. Failure to meet expectations could lead to harsh punishments, even though the failure was usually due to ignorance or a lack of training in the ways of their white enslavers.

In 1847, about a year after Lucy and Angeline arrived in Mississippi, Wineford Amanda, the minor heir of Reuben Higgs, also died at a tragically young age. John Higgs, the guardian of Reuben's remaining children, petitioned to have Wineford Amanda's slaves returned to Tennessee. Wheeless, Wineford Amanda's guardian, fought the petition, undoubtedly wanting to retain ownership of the slaves for himself. Ultimately, a judge ordered that the slaves be returned to Hardeman County, Tennessee. Lucy and her siblings were once again transferred in ownership to Reuben's other four children and their guardian John Higgs, and she moved back to Tennessee. Now only nine years old, another arduous journey and change of hands for Lucy and her siblings lay ahead. Many weeks must have separated the decision and the journey. It is difficult to imagine how a young child viewed the world, her work, and her family as the world threatened to change around her once again. There is no documentation about Lucy's life under the guardianship of Samuel Wheeless, especially after Wineford Amanda died. Having lost the battle to keep young Lucy and her siblings, did Wheeless's demeanor change? How did she pass the weeks knowing her life would be uprooted once more?

Lucy returned to the Higgs estate in Tennessee, presumably managed by the eldest of the brothers, and assimilated to a new life. Children on plantations were generally reared by the very old or young children in a communal setting. The conditions of their feeding, clothing, and care varied widely. Some children were raised on scarce protein, exhibiting signs of malnourishment, while others were offered plentiful portions. Some young enslaved children wore tunics or simple clothes, while others would be found roaming plantations naked. Some enslavers required children to work from a very young age. Once they reached working age, they would be given either the simple and practical clothes of fieldworkers or the more elevated attire of a houseworker.

Most enslaved young girls and boys in the South were working for the production of cash crops. With large-scale productions, farms were growing only a limited monoculture of some type. Cotton and tobacco were certainly among the most common and labor intensive—about

Inventory of the effects of Wineford Amanda Higgs, 1849.

fourteen pounds of tobacco was grown for every person in the United States in 1860—but there was a vast variety of crops grown and harvested by slave labor in Tennessee. Although the work was seasonal, they could be kept busy year-round, especially with the additional subsistence crops and livestock needed to feed a self-sufficient plantation.

As a young girl, Lucy had little time or energy to play. Typically, the only free time to recuperate both mentally and physically from their labors was evening, Sundays, and holidays. Leisure time is incredibly important for the development of young people but especially so for children in states of duress, such as forced labor. Free time was usually spent resting or doing household chores for the enslaved family but also in informal and formal social gatherings that allowed for the development of interpersonal skills. Some of these events were even organized by their enslavers who joined in on the festivities.

From an 1855 inventory of property, it seems that Lucy and Angeline(a) were reunited with Aaron, their older brother. Because young men were valuable in the slave trade, they were lucky to find he had not been sold for a hefty profit. The Higgs family estate was about 625 acres, large enough to need the labor of many men, women, and children to keep up. It seems as though Marcus Higgs, the eldest remaining Higgs male heir, was the reigning sibling in charge of the estate, but that remains unclear. Meanwhile, records show that the extended Higgs family, including Reuben's brother Jacob, steadily increased his slave population, owning thirty-six slaves in 1850 and sixty-five in 1860. Since the properties were

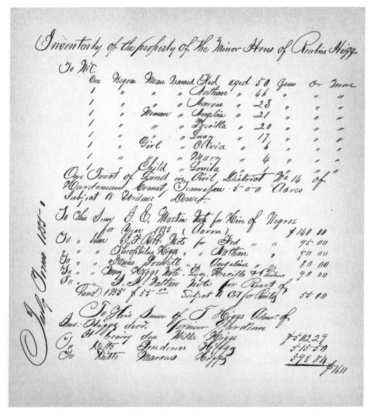

Inventory of the minor heirs of Reuben Higgs, 1855.

in close proximity, Lucy had a robust slave community with whom she could bond.

An 1855 inventory of property of the minor heirs of Reuben Higgs lists all of the enslaved people remaining in the possession of his estate. There were nine in total. There were three men: Ted, aged fifty or more; Nathan, forty-six; and Aaron, twenty-three. There were three women: Angeline(a), twenty-one; Priscilla, twenty; and Lucy, now seventeen. Three young children joined them: Olivia, six; Mary, four; and Louisa, only one year old. In 1855, Lucy was hired out, along with Priscilla and the children, for the sum of $90. Lucy could have been hired out for arduous plantation work while still in her teens.

On February 10, 1855, the Higgs family heirs, Martha Jane Higgs, Leanna Kennan (and Elijah Kennan by marriage), Theophilus Higgs, Mary M. Higgs, Wiley Higgs, Marcus Higgs, and Prudence Higgs, appeared before the court to petition for the sale of the Higgs family farm, numbering 625 acres, a large-scale farm for the time period, and "Mother Nancy," a bondswoman on the farm aged about twenty-eight years. The Higgs family holdings, while robust, were still small compared to other Halifax County families by this time—for scale, the family of Thomas Pollock Devereaux, who had $52,000 in land value and 580 people enslaved by 1850. After numerous legal negotiations and the death of Marcus in 1858, Wiley petitioned in 1860 that the remaining slaves be divided between him and the eldest remaining Higgs heir, Prudence, who was only fifteen years old at the time and under the guardianship of A. J. Campbell.

Around this same time period, in 1860, Lucy gave birth to a baby girl named Mona. Like all women, Black enslaved women also had the universal experiences of womanhood, including motherhood, marriage, rites of passage, and community with other women. Like her mother before her, Mona was born the property of the Higgs family. Mona became part of a profitable cycle of slave birthing that developed after the ban of the transatlantic slave trade in 1808. Prior to the ban, children and pregnant mothers were seen as a burden and financial risk for slave owners. After the ban of the transatlantic slave trade, however, slave motherhood became a profitable, monetized endeavor because it was the only way to increase the slave population to meet demand and increase profit. Motherhood became practically a requirement of enslaved women, and they had no bodily autonomy.

The identity of Mona's father is unknown. Some accounts of Lucy's life mention a "husband" during this time period, perhaps a fellow bondsman named Calvin or George Higgs. If they were married, they had to ask permission of their enslavers. Some slaveholders encouraged marriage and motherhood to uphold traditional gender conventions and order in addition to the financial benefits of childbearing. Some stories of marriages between slaves, such as Harriet and Joseph Berry of Virginia, who escaped enslavement during the Civil War, indicate that owners rejoiced in the occasion and might even throw a family celebration for the new couple. Others saw an antithetical relationship between slavery and marriage because exclusivity and permanence of legal marriage prohibited the ability to sell slaves and increase profits. Enslaved people had to receive permission to marry from their owners, and that permission did not protect them from being separated. The permission did not afford them any legal recognition of security for their marriage or family. As a civil contract, slaves could not partake because they had no civil standing. Marriage by mutual agreement had no legal ramifications or protections. Because enslaved people were the property of their masters, the master had primary right over his property. While it is likely that Calvin or George was the father of Lucy's child Mona, it was also common for marriages "abroad" to occur when enslaved people from different homesteads would unite. This arrangement offered an expanded pool of potential partners and ensured that they would not marry blood relatives unlike their southern white counterparts.

While the marriage laws differed for enslaved people, the functional aspects of marriage had important similarities with some critical adjustments. Enslaved people wanted, maybe even expected, to marry someone they loved and selected. But in some cases, masters forced marriages between slaves, while in other cases, they married for practical reasons. Men and women in slave marriages often assumed similar gender roles to their white counterparts. Men were often the "head of household," while women were subordinate and took on responsibilities for cooking, cleaning, and caring for children. However, because each situation was unique for slave families, the patriarchal system was adapted to help African American families survive and adapt their ideals and values to their circumstances.

Unfortunately, there is also the real possibility that Lucy's child Mona was fathered by her enslaver. The slaveholding household could be a place of sexual, physical, and psychological violence. It was not at all uncommon for the man of the household to engage in extramarital affairs with the slaves he owned, often openly and with the full knowledge of the remainder of the family. Children of slaves who were fathered by their masters were born as property, too, and treated in the same manner as the other slave property.

Enslaved women often formed a loose network of support that had many purposes. They disseminated information about birth control and abortion, for example. If the mother chose to move forward with pregnancy, the unofficial networks, which varied from place to place, provided Black healers who would use traditional methods of medicine to ensure the health of mother and child. They formed a community of women that surrounded Black women during their birthing and child-rearing process. Meanwhile, white slave holders had different motives and methods for tending to the reproductive health of their slaves during pregnancy and childbirth, increasingly involving white male doctors in the process. Those doctors were invested in fertility and childbirth as a way to facilitate the continued growth of the enslaved population and line the pockets of themselves and wealthy plantation owners. They denied the validity of women's knowledge of their own bodies and the social conventions of their community folkways. Women's bodies—through physical labor, childbirth, and nursing—were routinely exploited for the purpose of perpetuating the institution of slavery. Unfortunately, Lucy may have even been a victim of coerced procreation and arranged marriage. Some enslavers ensured that there were prospects for mates once a woman reached childbearing age. They might even incentivize marriage and childbearing with less arduous tasks, separate domestic living spaces, new clothes, and additional provisions in addition to little or no physical punishment.

Regardless of the conditions of conception, the birth of Mona was undoubtedly steeped with mixed emotions: the pride and joy of a new mother and the fear and sorrow of a life bound into slave labor. The birth of Mona offered Lucy the opportunity to love and be loved unconditionally. She experienced the instinct to protect her child. Lucy and Mona joined a group of enslaved people from her plantation and nearby properties that formed an unofficial and unsanctioned community that participated in communal activities between sundown and sunup, such as hunting, fishing, storytelling, music making, and dancing. Children also promised the relief of some labors as they aged, a help around the household for the enslaved mother, just like young children born to white parents in the nineteenth century promised to be a hand around a farm.

Before Lucy could settle into the rhythm of slave labor and motherhood, the Higgs family slaves were divided again in 1861. Prudence, only seventeen years of age, was granted ownership of twenty-two-year-old Lucy and Mona, while Lucy's siblings were given to Wylie. Prudence lived on the property originally owned by Reuben and Elizabeth, and Lucy returned to the site of her youngest childhood memories. Prudence eventually bought out Wiley, reuniting Reuben Higgs's remaining people in bondage. Meanwhile, the Civil War was brewing, and slave owners were clinging to a waning way of life in the South.

2

PRUDENCE AND ESCAPE

Prudent: (adjective) acting with or showing care and thought for the future.

SOME HISTORIANS ARGUE THAT THE CIVIL WAR WAS NOT ABOUT slavery but about states' rights and the economy. Undoubtedly, those were among the issues that motivated the Civil War. But the Civil War was, at its core, ultimately about the institution of slavery. As abolitionist Frederick Douglass so astutely predicted in *Douglass' Monthly* in 1861, "The American people and the Government at Washington may refuse to recognize it for a time . . . that the war now being waged in this land is a war for and against slavery; and that it can never be effectually put down till one or the other of these vital forces is completely destroyed." Proslavery advocates saw slaves as an extended family of their owners, but, ultimately, enslaved people were property that was held, bought, exchanged, and discarded based on the economic gains associated with their labor. Southern plantations were businesses that made calculated economic decisions based on the size of their crop and the number of hands they had to cultivate the land. The rights of property owners in the

South and the economic gains or losses they experienced were inextricably yoked to slavery.

It is important to remember that Abraham Lincoln, although opposed to slavery as unjust, was not an abolitionist and was comparably moderate in his antislavery position compared to his more liberal Republican counterparts. His main goal was to keep slavery out of the Western Territories. Lincoln's election in 1860 did signal to southerners that the institution of slavery was at risk. By February 1861, legislators of the seven southern states of South Carolina, Mississippi, Florida, Alabama, Georgia, Louisiana, and Texas had voted to secede from the United States of America, forming the Confederate States of America, electing Jefferson Davis of Mississippi as their president. They created a constitution including states' rights that protected the system of slavery. Aggravated by Lincoln's management of conflict at Fort Sumter in South Carolina, four additional slaveholding states joined the Confederacy: Arkansas, North Carolina, Tennessee, and Virginia.

Many early historians of the Civil War practically erased the contributions of Black soldiers and volunteers, claiming the enslaved had gained freedom with absolutely no effort. Many Union soldiers fought to preserve the Union, not to end slavery. Although many Yankee soldiers disagreed with having Black soldiers join their ranks, the Union did eventually accept Black men into their army and navy. More than 178,000 Black men served in the Union military, or about 12 percent of forces, and they suffered a disproportionate number of casualties. The number of Black cooks, laundresses, and other volunteers who supported the war effort is innumerable.

While the Civil War was brewing, Lucy, her child Mona, and Lucy's siblings (and perhaps a husband) were at work on Prudence Higgs's farm. Perhaps reuniting with family would finally give Lucy the courage and strength, mixed with audacious hope, to seek a better future for her and Mona. Lucy's days were spent laboring in the home and field for the Higgs family and providing care for Mona as she could without disrupting her duties. Lucy probably strapped young Mona to her back as she worked in the fields or in the home, weighing her options.

In smaller operations, like Prudence Higgs's, where families owned fewer than twenty slaves, most enslaved workers did a variety of jobs. In addition to domestic work, most slaves working in a smaller operation would work alongside their white male masters who could monitor their productivity directly. On larger plantations or perhaps one owned by a woman, an overseer or estate manager was hired to oversee labor. They might use gang labor to work sunup to sundown at a rigorous pace, especially if they grew tobacco, which required a great deal of constant attention. It is not clear what kind of crops were grown at the Higgs family estate. Only a very small percentage of enslaved women had non-fieldwork. Seeking to maximize their economic gains, planters required laborers to work in all conditions year-round. The humid and hot conditions in Tennessee coupled with cold-resistant variations of crops meant that workers would need to tend the field in all temperatures. While many of the experiences of slaves differed according to the crops they cultivated, the cyclical nature of planting did give most slaves some shared labor experiences. A cycle of plowing, planting, weeding, and harvesting was almost universal, and the harvest was the most arduous. Once harvested, the crops had to be ginned, threshed, cured, or ground. Between parts of the cycle, slaves would be put to other productive tasks inside and outside the home. The work was relentless.

The style of slave management depended not only on the type of crop and farm size but also on the disposition of the owner and the crop they harvested. On the farm of Prudence Higgs, who remained unmarried until after the Civil War (she married Albert Cheairs in 1866), Lucy might have experienced a different lifestyle at the hands of her mistress than many of her counterparts at other plantations with a male head of household. If she was fortunate, she might build a relationship with her mistress and go on to take a privileged position in the household that required fewer hours of backbreaking field labor. She might have been the recipient of a more benevolent mistress who gave her plenty of rations with sufficient protein, functional clothing, and a reasonable place to sleep. She may even have had Sundays off. There were certainly cases of such owners.

However, Prudence Higgs could exercise the same legal rights to punish her slaves through physical violence as any male owner. There is no recorded evidence of this in any accounts of Lucy's life, but the probability of some brutality is high. Like her younger half-sibling Wineford Amanda, Prudence learned about managing slaves from her parents and developed her own style of management and punishment. Lucy may have endured lashings for minor misdeeds or more serious broken bones or other injuries for more egregious errors. Some masters beat their slaves to death for disrespecting their superiority and status. If this was the type of household in which Lucy lived, fear must have pervaded her daily life.

Another fear that permeated slave existence was the threat of being separated from family. Perhaps it was in her domestic duties in the house that Lucy got wind of rumors that they might be sold farther south. Every enslaved person knew what being "sold down the river" meant: a lifetime of hard labor on southern cotton plantations and the very real threat of being separated from family. If Lucy stayed on the farm to await her fate, she might have been carted to nearby Memphis, the center of slave trafficking in the Upper South.

In 1808, America banned the importation of slaves from abroad, so the domestic slave trade by ship along the coast became very lucrative. The upper Mississippi region benefited because it was well situated to supply the lower Mississippi trade along the coastline. The slave export business could be even more profitable than the labor of the slave on the farm. In the nineteenth century, more than 60 percent of the Black enslaved population were forcibly moved through the trafficking of slaves. Between 1820 and 1860, more than 1 million people were shipped across state lines. Most transfers were on foot and were not recorded, but ships had to record on manifestos their captives by name. The threat of being separated from family was crushing. Some 40 percent of slaves transported via ship were without any family. Of the remainder, more than 65 percent of families were split up for sale. In total, a staggering estimated 88 percent of families were forcibly separated from their immediate families if they were sold "down South." Lucy, her husband, and her young child could have become collateral of the profitable financial exchange of human life.

Not only were they faced with the possibility of sale, but enslaved people were also forced or coerced into the Confederate war effort. Some took noncombat roles, such as musicians, labor to build fortifications, railroad workers, hospital staff, cooks, and buriers of the dead. They even took manufacturing jobs to allow white men of the Confederacy to do battle. Because the vast majority of the population of the South was Black and the population of the North was much larger, the distribution of labor was essential to the Confederate war effort.

At some point in the summer of 1862, Lucy got wind that Prudence Higgs intended to sell Lucy and her family "down South." What motivated Prudence Higgs's potential sale of Lucy and her family after so many legal battles to obtain ownership is unclear, but perhaps she wanted to capitalize on the monetary value of her property before the war stripped them of their status as property. Lucy (and perhaps her husband Calvin) promised to bring in a considerable sum as able-bodied and skilled young people who would have sold for high sums at auction. Lucy would be especially valuable as she entered into fertility. Prudence probably wanted to take advantage of the moment before war broke out. It was not uncommon for women to participate in the sale of their enslaved people, but they did not do so directly because the slave auction sites and dealings were the domain of white men. Women who wanted to sell their human property had to enlist the help of the men in their lives to do the buying and selling for them because the brutal and sexually charged atmosphere of the slave markets was no place for a lady. Since Prudence's brothers were still living on the family property, they may have been a logical proxy for the sale. Maybe Lucy overheard Prudence and Wylie discussing the fate of her and her family over dinner at the dining room table. The process of buying or selling human bodies began at the home well before reaching the auction block or slave pen. For Prudence, a white, unmarried, slaveholding woman who lived on an isolated plot of land, emancipating slaves threatened her entire prospect of financial independence and social status within the community. She may have recognized that defeat in the Civil War also meant the loss of her economic security.

Whatever the motivations were for Prudence's threat of sale, the prospect was unbearable for Lucy and her fellow slaves. In June 1862, Lucy and her friends and family hatched a plan to escape. Little is known about exactly what transpired. It is likely they had a specific destination in mind, for they would fortunately find protection nearby. They had no guarantee of safety, knowing slaves were routinely caught and returned to their enslavers. The darkness of night offered modest cover, and the stars gave them some guidance on their flight. But the dark night may also obscure familiar details of the nearby woods they needed to deter their owners and deflect detection. How many people were with their party, and did they have any help from kind strangers along their path? What courage was required to steal away in the middle of the night with only enough supplies they could carry on their backs. Mona was only two or three years of age then, a bright-eyed and merry child whose sweet chatter or loud wails of fear could jeopardize their escape.

In the sweltering heat of a Tennessee summer, Lucy swaddled Mona in her gown and snuck away under the cover of night. Long after the lights were extinguished in the home of her enslavers, her brave party of fellow freedom seekers took off on a three-mile journey under the light of the stars in an ink-blue sky. The stars had long provided a celestial road map for those escaping bondage on the unofficial routes of the Underground Railroad. From Gray's Creek through woods, overgrown fields, and hostile territory, they found the Indiana 23rd Volunteer Regiment encamped at the fairgrounds just north of Bolivar, Tennessee, which was under martial law. Later reminiscences from nostalgic soldiers inflated Lucy's trek to thirty miles. They arrived "dusty and footsore from the long and hurried journey," according to Major Shadrach Hooper, who recalled the events of Lucy's escape for a newspaper more than thirty years later.

Having escaped the plantation and braved the three-mile journey to arrive at the feet of the Indiana 23rd Regiment, Lucy and the others who escaped with her pleaded for their protection, fearing that her enslaver would kill them. An unidentified man even came to the camp and tried to collect the fugitives. Perhaps it was Wylie Higgs who chased them down given that they belonged to Prudence, then only seventeen and unmarried. In a slave state in the Deep South, Lucy and her fellow freedom seekers took a great risk in fleeing. They were considered property, and the Fugitive Slave Act of 1850 required that any citizen return slave property to their owners, often for a handsome reward. The retaliation of owners against slaves who attempted to escape could be brutal. One account from Captain Tyler Reid of the 3rd Massachusetts Cavalry describes finding a young girl, about Lucy's age, bound by a rusted iron yoke in a small cabin room. She had been there for three months—emaciated with gaping wounds and festering conditions. She was being held there by a female mistress, Madame Coutreil, as punishment for attempted escape and supposed Yankee sympathies during the Union occupation of New Orleans in 1862. Mistress slave owners often showed no tolerance for insubordination, and Lucy could have faced a fate as dreadful.

The soldiers of the Indiana 23rd provided protection for the fugitives despite the Fugitive Slave Act of 1850 thanks to the precedent of Union general Benjamin Butler. In 1861, Butler was presented with a challenge. Three enslaved men—Shepard Mallory, James Townsend, and Frank Baker—escaped and sought protection at Union Fort Monroe in Hampton, Virginia. The men had been working as slaves to build weapons for the Confederate soldiers. Butler knew that the men, had they been returned to the slaveholder, would continue to make weapons and support the Confederate cause. So he identified a loophole in the Fugitive Slave Act, which identified enslaved people as property. The Union army could already claim enemy property that helped the war effort. Butler was clever; he called the men "contraband of war," and they were allowed to stay at Fort Monroe, later known as the Grand Contraband Camp. Other contraband camps cropped up across Union-held lands, operating more like small towns.

The policy of accepting fugitives as contraband was not entirely benevolent, however. Taking slaves out of the workforce in the South weakened the Confederacy and helped the Union cause, and they remained property under law. The plan provided a middle-ground policy that did not significantly interfere with slavery but also allowed for the fluctuating political landscape. General Butler did not return slaves, nor did he free them. He also did not break any laws. The Fugitive Slave Act, which required the return of property, was a Union law, and because he was in a seceded southern state, he did not have to abide by that law. He could warrant taking human property as contraband of war to support the Union cause.

The Senate met in extraordinary session from July 4 to August 6, 1861. One of the wartime measures it considered was the Confiscation Act. The act was designed to allow the federal government to seize property, including slave property, being used to support the Confederate rebellion. The Senate passed the final bill on August 5, 1861, by a vote of twenty-four to eleven, and it was signed into law by President Lincoln the next day. Although this bill had symbolic importance, it had little effect on the rebellion or wartime negotiations. Senator Lyman Trumball of Illinois introduced another, more comprehensive bill, the Confiscation Act of 1862, that allowed for the confiscation of Confederate property regardless of whether it had been used to support the rebellion. Radical Republicans rallied behind the bill, while more conservative politicians feared federal overreach and denying property owners their constitutional rights. Finally, a group of moderate senators drafted a compromise bill that authorized the federal government to free slaves in conquered rebel territory and prohibited the return of fugitive slaves, such as Lucy and her fellow enslaved people.

Perhaps it was the passing of these bills that spooked Prudence into selling her property, anticipating that the arrival of Union troops in Bolivar would inevitably result in the confiscation of her property. It was sell, or lose everything. While there were certainly cases of slaves being returned to owners with healthy payouts as rewards, women who owned slaves, such as Prudence, would need to rely on male kin or employees to apprehend the fugitives. She may have predicted that her brother Wylie would soon be joining the secessionists and leave her with few options to retrieve her assets. The April 1862 Act for the Release of Certain Persons Held to Service or Labor in the District of Columbia, which offered compensation to slaveholders who were loyal to the Union, did not apply to Prudence because her family were secessionists. Although hundreds of women slaveholders did appear to apply for compensation under the act, Prudence's only consolation was the Confederate Congress's act drafted in response that stipulated that if the Confederacy won, the act would require the Union states to pay for the losses of property value.

The first semiofficial legislation for emancipation came as early as August 30, 1861, by General John C. Fremont, an 1856 Republican candidate for president. Putting Missouri under martial law, he proclaimed that the enslaved people belonging to the rebels were confiscated property and thereby freed. This premature emancipation was not appreciated by President Lincoln, who feared that the indecisive border states would get apprehensive and join the Confederacy if they deemed the outcome would be the mass release of a population "unprepared for freedom." Again and again, Lincoln ensured the return of "fugitives from service or labor." Contraband, on the other hand, was much more comfortable for conservatives, who felt at ease thinking of Black men and women as property, especially in service of winning the Union victory. In April 1862, the Senate and House of Representatives passed the Act for the Release of Certain Persons Held to Service or Labor in the District of Columbia, which stated that

> all persons held to service or labor within the District of Columbia by reason of African descent are hereby discharged and freed of and from all claim to such service or labor; and from and after the passage of this act neither slavery nor involuntary servitude, except for crime, whereof the party shall be duly convicted, shall hereafter exist in said District.

Sadly, this did not apply to Lucy and her kin, who fell outside the jurisdiction of the act, but perhaps its passage fueled their bravery to mount an escape and hope for better future outcomes.

It is impossible to know what Lucy and her fellow freedom seekers understood about the policies enacted or the risk they undertook in seeking the safety of the Indiana 23rd on that fateful evening. Perhaps they had heard about the contraband camps from the people in their enslaved community in nearby plantations. Or maybe one of them caught wind of the Indiana 23rd encampment in one of those rare moments when slaves would be allowed to go into nearby towns to barter and trade and get supplies. Escaping enslavement only to enter into the unpredictable contraband life was akin to making a bet that the Union forces would be sympathetic and ultimately victorious, or else Lucy and her compatriots would suffer the consequences of being returned to their enslavers. They risked stumbling on a regiment that strictly enforced the Fugitive Slave Act, rejecting requests to join camps or returning escapees to their owners. Some Union soldiers stole from enslaved people, raped, and brutalized them. Ultimately, Lucy and her fellow freedom seekers were among the 500,000 men, women, and children who fled enslavement in search of protection under the Union troops. Their collective resistance helped to undermine and dismantle the institution of slavery.

The Indiana 23rd Regiment was stationed in Bolivar, Tennessee—Confederate territory. According to the wartime letters of Captain Benjamin F. Walter to his sister Maggie, the local white population was prosperous, and the region was well developed in comparison to many other areas of Tennessee they had seen, perhaps due to proximity to the railroad. He noted the ambivalence the locals had toward the Union soldiers, supposedly appreciative of their gentlemanliness compared to the Confederate troops who came before them. Another account from a soldier in Bolivar generously calls the rebels "misguided brothers" who must be brought back "tenderly" to account for their "damnable treason." The sentiments were mixed, though, as one soldier declared, "The time for kind words and gentle treatment has passed. Nothing but hard blows and loss of property will ever do any good." This is a common theme in the newspaper correspondence from the regiment—they were no longer interested in fighting a gentlemanly and kind war.

The *New Albany Daily Ledger* printed a letter dated June 18, 1862, from an unidentified soldier of the Indiana 23rd Regiment to his wife in the city. He writes, "Bolivar is a very handsome town, but the people, especially the women, are terribly secesh," meaning they were ardent secessionists. He recalls a group of young men who went to serenade a young woman who declined their advances: "Yankee music has no charms for the Southern Blood." In contrast, he writes, "Our troops met with a very different reception from the colored people, who received them with open arms, and it is with great difficulty that they can be prevented from following the army."

The troops were met with "squads" of Black residents as they marched by with "exclamations and questions." Many Black enslaved people sought out the troop in search of sanctuary. Walter wrote that contrabands were "generally returned to their owners," however, despite the passage of the Confiscation Act. There is no mention of any specific command policy on the matter, but he cites specific incidents of freedom seekers being returned. Walter wrote, "The negroes generally, which I have met, are remarkably intelligent and truthful, being pretty well posted in regard to the state of affairs in the southern confederacy, knowing far more about them than their masters suspect, although they have endeavored to keep their slaves ignorant." Lucy and her fellow escapees were both well informed and lucky that the sentiment changed in the regiment, and they were admitted into the protection of the troop.

According to secondhand accounts many years later, Lucy arrived with her husband, who eventually enlisted in the United States Colored Troops (USCT), though no legal documentation of their marriage survives. An army officer in Louisiana wrote in 1863 to the *Boston Transcript* about the conditions of the men who had escaped enslavement and resided in Black camps. He says that there were "models of neatness and order" and that they were rarely punished for misconduct. However, he witnessed that less than half were passed for volunteer service by the surgeons because of their health and condition. Very few were without marks from "severe lashing," and nearly half were rejected from disabilities arising from lash whippings and dog bites on their legs and thighs.

By August 4, 1862, the rebels were encroaching on the regiment in Bolivar. According to reports to the hometown newspaper, the regiment had taken on about 150 to 200 Black workers who were busy building fortifications. They marched in two ranks, followed by a makeshift marching band. Armed with sticks for guns, the soldier described the Black workers as a "jolly crew" that was civil and satisfied and never came around the camp.

The Union soldiers had mixed feelings about the service of Black men in the army. One article, printed on the one-year occasion of the regiment's deployment, expresses these serious rifts in beliefs and the complexity with which the motives of the Civil War can be clearly summarized:

> The institution of slavery must be eradicated from the Union, and that traitors must be made to feel that in embracing treason they have forfeited to the Government everything they possess, and if they be spared, they breathe only through the mercy of that Government.

Lest the Union soldier be mistaken as wholly benevolent in his efforts, he goes on to clarify,

> But the question arises, as this institution of slavery is the life of the rebellion, shall we in support of the Constitution arm the slaves against their traitor masters? God forbid. We enlisted in this war to save the Constitution, without any desire to interfere with slavery. The Constitution was framed by white men for their descendents. It gives no rights to the negro: it grants to him no priveleges; we do not therefore desire the he should defend it. As the worthy sons of noble sires, never, no never, will we descend to ask the assistance of the negro to defend our glorious heritage.

But it was perfectly acceptable to put Black men and women to labor in defense of the Constitution and that glorious heritage. He goes on, "The slaves are here employed in throwing up breastworks and erecting fortifications, and other menial labors. . . . It would be advantageous to detail a certain number, say four for each company, to cook, clean quarters, etc." And this is how Lucy began her service to the regiment—as a laundress, seamstress, and cook. As she proved her loyalty and ability, she worked her way up to the rank of nurse, a privileged position held almost exclusively by middle-class white women.

3
LIFE AS A REGIMENTAL "NURSE"

THOSE WHO FLED FROM SOUTHERN PLANTATIONS TO SEEK PROTECTION of the Union soldiers could seek out one of the several contraband camps established throughout the heart of war territory. These makeshift camps became a refuge for hundreds of thousands of people. Camps had squalid conditions and meager rations, while people lived in constant fear of raids from white southerners. Despite these unsavory conditions, camps concentrated large groups of people who could exchange ideas, reunite with family, and even foster educational opportunities.

Although there were a number of camps throughout Tennessee, Lucy instead joined about 100 "contrabands" or "refugees," as they were called, who worked directly for the Indiana 23rd Volunteer Regiment and traveled with the troop. As contraband of war, Lucy, Calvin, and any other escapees from the Higgs farm were put to work right away. While Colonel William L. Sanderson described the refugees in a letter to his daughter as "hard at work, cheerful and happy," the reality was, in many ways, a different kind of bondage that required work in exchange for protection, provisions, and the potential for freedom.

The formerly enslaved who reached a camp or troop could begin to imagine a better future, but emancipation was a slow experience. Contraband laws did offer space within Union lines and protection for people escaping enslavement to survive outside the reach of their owners, but they were not legally granted freedom, and little about their daily lives looked like freedom. This was called a "transition state" by many during the time—a period between bondage and an unknown future. Some even compared this transition phase to the Old Testament in Exodus when the Israelites escaped slavery in Egypt, enduring suffering on the way to the Holy Land. In fact, they referred to themselves often as "refugees." The entire system was deemed a military "necessity" because, ultimately, the Union forces wanted to make sure that Black labor was used not in service to the Confederacy but rather in support of Union forces.

It is impossible to know if Lucy and her fellow freedom seekers knew about the troops stationed at Bolivar before they escaped. It is impossible to know if she was aware of the contraband laws that protected her from recapture. It is also impossible to know if she chose this path out of a sense of duty or desperation or perhaps both. How could she care for young Mona without the provisions afforded by the regiment? Where could she run if not for the camp of the Indiana 23rd? What qualities of Lucy and her peers made the soldiers take them in rather than turn them away?

THE INDIANA 23RD REGIMENT

By the time Lucy reached the regiment, they had already been active for nearly a year. An infantry was generally structured with the following: a corps, a division, a brigade, a regiment, and a company. The most important for the infantryman was the regiment because he closely identified with it, and, especially at the beginning of the war, all ten companies of about 100 soldiers each came from the same town or county. The Indiana 23rd Regiment, who signed up for what they believed was a three- to six-month period that later turned into years, was assigned to rendezvous at the old fairgrounds in New Albany, Indiana, later known as Camp Noble.

The local newspaper, the *New Albany Daily Ledger*, heralded their early morning departure on August 15, 1861. The streets were lined with sentimental families and sounded with martial music. The new recruits, laden with heavy knapsacks stuffed with personal belongings, marched

This 23rd Indiana Regiment (Blue Standard) flag was provided to the regiment by the citizens of New Albany, Indiana, for the price of $90 in 1862. Courtesy of the Indiana War Memorial Commission.

down Market Street in New Albany to gather in the public square, where they were presented with a banner by the women of the city featuring the thirty-four stars, the symbol of a unified country that was, for many, the core cause of the war. They walked several more miles to Jeffersonville, Indiana, where they embarked on the train to Indianapolis. They arrived after midnight and trekked another couple miles to camp. This was just the beginning of their four-year wartime journey, largely on foot. The next day, they boarded a train to St. Louis and marched further. They remained there for a few weeks, gaining valuable soldier training before leaving for the field in Paducah, Kentucky, arriving on September 11, 1861.

In Paducah, the men experienced their first taste of combat and military life. According to Shadrach Hooper's 1910 recollection of the regiment's war experience in Paducah,

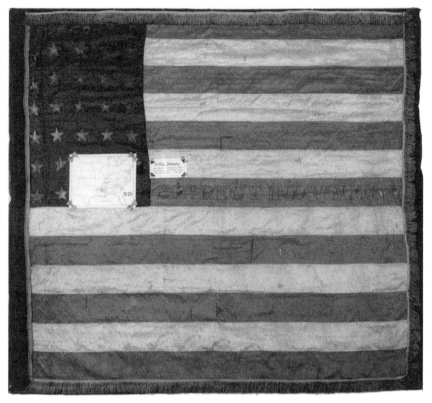

The 23rd Indiana Regiment national flag. Courtesy of the Indiana War Memorial Commission.

The service was constant and warlike, picket duty was exacting and arduous during the winter, and night alarms were frequent and exciting, all of which, together with one or two small skirmishes with the guerillas, enured men to the hardships of grim-visaged war and placed the regiment in the list of seasoned troops.

From Paducah, the regiment was called to assist in the battle of Belmont, Missouri. An arduous march, they were on foot for more than twenty-four hours with only short thirty-minute breaks to rest. By the time they reached Belmont, the battle had already concluded, and they immediately marched back to Paducah the same day. Colonel Sanderson withdrew the men finally at midnight to allow them to eat and rest for six hours before they continued the trek. On the return march, the men shed many of their personal belongings—extra clothing, bedding, toiletries, utensils, and any other superfluous comforts were discarded. What remained were the most treasured of personal items and the necessities, such as gun, cartridge box, blanket, canteen, and haversack (a one-shoulder knapsack).

They bided their time in Paducah for several months, constructing fortifications. They were called to action on January 2, 1862, convoyed by the gunboat *Conestoga* to the Tennessee and Cumberland rivers near Fort Henry and Fort Hieman. A skirmish ensued between the Union *Conestoga* soldiers and the Confederate forces along the banks of the rivers. While the campaign was brief, conditions were arduous. The men endured the "January thaw," a rise in the bayous and streams. Men, wagons, and artillery were mired by mud and streams that were waist deep. Hooper reflected, "While the entire distance going and returning was scarcely 150 miles, yet it required the greatest effort, constant labor and much suffering to complete the journey in twelve days."

After another return to base in Paducah, the regiment once again boarded steamers on February 2, 1862, headed for Forts Henry and Donelson in the battle that gave future president Grant the nickname "Unconditional Surrender." It was the first major Union victory and opened access to the heart of the Confederacy. On the morning of February 6, the command captured Fort Heiman, and gunboats battered Fort Henry, where the Confederate soldiers waved the white flag of surrender. Between the fall of Fort Henry and the surrender at Fort Donelson on February 16, the Indiana 23rd held Fort Henry. While they did not battle at Fort Donelson, they did experience severe weather, with six-inch snowfalls and freezing nights, and had little more than ordinary clothes for more than a week to keep them warm.

On March 14, they proceeded via steamer up the Tennessee River to Crump's Landing, about five miles from Pittsburg Landing, in preparation for what would later be known as the Battle of Shiloh. They marched the five miles to "Stony Lonesome" under a torrential downpour and lightning. By this point, they all scrapped their gray cadet uniform for the quintessential Union blue shirt and "camp-kettle" hat because the Confederates had adopted a gray uniform. Hooper recalls that the regiment lamented this change, as they were proud of their appearances, supposedly unexcelled by any other regiment in service.

The Battle of Shiloh was fought on April 6 and 7, 1862. The Indiana 23rd Regiment was under the command of General Wallace, and they reached the grounds late in the night after the first day of battle. The next morning, at 5:00 a.m., the Indiana 9th Battery, supported by the Indiana 23rd, opened engagement and remained under heavy fire and skirmish until evening. The battery lost one officer, and fifty-one soldiers were killed or wounded.

ARRIVAL IN BOLIVAR, TENNESSEE

The Indiana 23rd remained on the battlefield at Shiloh until April 17, when they were moved to participate in the siege of Corinth, Mississippi. They were soon pulled away again to an outpost in Bolivar, Tennessee, where they spent the summer. Colonel William L. Sanderson described the scene in Bolivar in a letter to his daughter:

> The enemy flees ahead of us, we make only very few prisoners, the people look ahead at us suspiciously here, because hier [*sic*] everything belongs to the rebels, the houses are ordinarily locked up and nothing can be seen but colored people who cry hurrah as soon as we march by.

By the time Lucy had reached the Indiana 23rd in Bolivar, they were a seasoned veteran regiment. They had seen battle, encountered harsh conditions, lost lives, endured sickness and wounds, and secured victories. Hooper's recollection of the events some fifty years later acknowledges the hardships of the soldiers and documents their movements and battles. While these soldiers on the battlefield often get the glory and recognition, they also required the support of innumerable volunteers, both officially sanctioned and unofficial, to survive the years of battle. Lucy and her fellow contraband were among those "volunteers" in the army.

Lucy had some federally sanctioned protections in the Confiscation Acts of 1861 and 1862, but they were loosely enforced. However, individuals within troops who were responsible for the care of refugees often felt

Major Shadrach Hooper.

a commitment to duty even if not personally committed to abolitionist causes. At the very least, the army had promised to protect refugees from gratuitous bodily harm in the form of rations and shelter. They promised to shield the escapees from their enslavers, and many individuals felt compelled to uphold that promise even if begrudgingly. It may have been the presence of little Mona that helped ensure Lucy and her fellow freedomseekers' safety with the regiment. In some contraband camps, children made up as much as half of the population of refugees. Children were often given special treatment, an outgrowth of increasingly senti-mental views of childhood in the nineteenth century. At the same time, aid organizations that came to contraband camps devised ways to compel young children into wage labor.

A general description of the conditions for contrabands in the camps may be gleaned from a questionnaire that was circulated to camp super-intendents in early 1863 by Chaplain John Eaton Jr., the general super-intendent of contrabands under Grant. Superintendents reported that their clothing was "very indifferent" and that they lived in "board cabins" guarded by both soldiers and "colored police." Pneumonia and measles circulated among the inhabitants, and they worked "building fortifica-tions, cutting wood, rolling logs, running sawmills in the Quartermas-ter's Department and Hospitals." They were lauded for their piety and commended for their bravery and readiness to be soldiers. All of them claimed a fear of going South or severe treatment or a desire for liberty.

MEET THE GRESHAMS

After a visual physical exam of their health and whether they were able-bodied for labor, the men were usually put to manual labor, while the women were put into the positions of laundress and cook for the troops. A correspondent with the Indiana 23rd reported back to the hometown New Albany newspaper,

> It is amusing to see the negroes as they go to and from their work on fortifications. There are about 150 or 200, and they march along in two ranks, following a martial band, consisting of an old snare drum with one head and the hoops cracked, a cane fife, and a pair of bones. Some

of them are armed with sticks for guns, and a more jolly crew you never saw. They work well, and save the soldiers many a hard day's work. They are very civil, and never come around the camps, and I never saw a set of fellows better satisfied.

Lucy was part of the 200-person-strong rank that marched with the Indiana 23rd. She did not stay at the contraband camps in Bolivar, and she distinguished herself in service to the regiment. She was assigned the job of laundress and cook.

These tasks were likely familiar to Lucy, having been at the service of the Higgs family. But now her job was immeasurably bigger, and the tasks were arduous. One week's laundry for a typical family required fifty gallons of hot water, which required hauling firewood and stoking a fire. Heavily soiled clothes had to be soaked overnight, and it is certain a soldier's uniform was heavily soiled. Clothes were removed from one bin after scrubbing and boiling and added to another bin to rinse and then wring and hang on a clothesline. The process was relentless, especially with variables of weather, labor, and supplies. As a cook, Lucy would have worked under a head cook trained and appointed by the Sanitary Commission, but she would have been responsible for preparing for meals in much the same way she had as an enslaved woman on Prudence's farm. Union soldiers were fed pork or beef, coffee, sugar, salt, vinegar, and sometimes dried fruits and vegetables. They were given hard biscuits in lean times to stave off hunger. All signs indicate that Lucy was an industrious and dedicated laborer, and her work would be recognized.

During the war, Lucy met General William Quintin (W. Q.) Gresham, whose wife accompanied him in the camp. The Greshams came from Lanesville, Indiana, and General Gresham was a rising political star who eventually became secretary of state under Grover Cleveland. According to one source, Lucy was assigned the task of waiting on General Gresham's wife, born Matilda McGrain. They apparently became quite close, building a lifelong relationship that would last well past the war into the 1890s. Despite what sounds like a very amiable, perhaps even loving, relationship between Lucy and the Greshams, the Greshams

Lucy served General W. Q. Gresham and his wife during her time with the Indiana 23rd. She would go on to work in his home in New Albany, Indiana, after the Civil War. Photograph from "Presidential Possibilities," *The Illustrated American,* September 5, 1891.

held complicated political beliefs. Their opinions about the rights of Black Americans cast a shadow over their relationship with Lucy.

Matilda McGrain was born in Louisville, Kentucky, just across the river from New Albany, to an extreme proslavery father with eight children and several slaves. The children and household were cared for by enslaved men and women, and Matilda describes her father's management of the bondspeople as lacking "cruelty" or "severity." She describes the manumission of an enslaved man, Horace, owned by their father, who bought his freedom and went on to be a superintendent at a colored Sunday school. Matilda's father eventually formed the opinion that slavery was bad for the economy—a less profitable form of property than land. He bought a farm in Indiana, a free state, but remained an ardent secessionist.

In contrast, W. Q. Gresham's mother was steadfastly opposed to slavery if not a true abolitionist. She actively shared stories with her young children of the evils of slavery and expressed great pride that her father chose to move to Indiana, a free state. Her moral feelings about slavery influenced Gresham's political ideologies. However, Gresham's pre–Civil War, antislavery views were largely politically and economically motivated. He focused on the preservation of the Union and upholding federal power—not the abolition of slavery on moral grounds. Gresham was not fighting the Civil War to end slavery; he was fighting to preserve the Union because he believed that, as Matilda recalls, "if the Union could be held together, the growth and development of the country and public opinion would, in time, bring about the abolition of slavery without violence and bloodshed, and with compensation to the slaveholders."

Matilda Gresham's biography of W. Q. Gresham leans heavily into the difference between a Republican, his party of choice, and an abolitionist, whom she describes with some vitriol. She writes,

> The Republicans—at least those Republicans with whom I was closely associated—believed slavery would be so restricted that public sentiment would, without violence or bloodshed, bring about in time abolition, but with compensation to the slave owner. On the other hand, the Abolitionists' platform was "immediate and unconditional abolition." They claimed that fairness and good faith precluded the interpretation of the Constitution in the light of the Declaration of Independence, for the fathers who drew the Constitution intended it should be a pro-slavery instrument. But because it was immoral they would not obey it.

W. Q. Gresham believed that "freeing a slave did not elevate that slave to citizenship." His goal was to promote antislavery without agitating the South. He actively worked to "abate" the Underground Railroad in Indiana and had many proslavery friends whom he always considered in his political opinions. Even when it came to the Fugitive Slave Act of 1850, which mandated the return of escaped slaves to their owners, Gresham was very moderate in his opinion, neither outright supporting nor outright criticizing the provisions. "In short," Matilda writes, "Walter Q. Gresham was never an Abolitionist."

For the wealthy wife of a political leader and lawyer, Matilda was accustomed to a certain lifestyle of ease. Apparently, she needed to maintain aspects of that lifestyle while accompanying her husband in war. Lucy took on the role of servant for Matilda Gresham, unpaid for her labor, even in a war that presumably sought to free her from bondage. As "contraband" of war, she was still the property of the troop that she accompanied, and she made herself useful. Matilda writes without remorse that her childhood cook Winnie, or "Old Winn," was free in Indiana but enslaved in Kentucky. Matilda naively believed Winnie preferred to be in Kentucky, saying, "'Old Winn' preferred Kentucky to living under the reactionary Indiana constitution." Winnie served Matilda through her marriage in 1858, only four years before Lucy began her service with Matilda on the front. If her biography of her husband is any indication, Matilda was very intelligent, and she paid close attention to the political landscape. She had a subtle understanding of, for example, the *Dred Scott* case, the Lincoln and Douglass debates, and the Fugitive Slave Act of 1850. As she infuses her personal opinions into the biography, it's easy to see she was not an outright abolitionist, either, and she was more than willing to utilize enslaved people for her labor and comfort.

Lucy was a very capable servant to the Greshams and a cook and laundress for the other soldiers. She was greatly admired for her honesty, integrity, and intelligence. She was unfailingly generous with her time and services. Soldiers recalled she was always willing to sew on a button, patch trousers, or make delicacies around the campfire—small kindnesses that reminded the men of home and endeared them to Lucy. The men of the regiment often bitterly complained about a lack of access to newspapers and letters from home. Lucy offered them some consoling as they mended and yearned for news from home.

To provide these little luxuries for the men and the basic necessities for her and Mona, Lucy was an industrious forager. She was able to scrounge up fabric for her own clothes, utensils, and simple natural medicines and was always equipped with a washboard and tub. Menial as these tasks may seem, the men noticed her value and recall with great gratitude for many years the love and service she provided.

Nurse Lucy

Once Lucy's skills were recognized, she was called to a higher purpose in the ranks. The regiment's surgeon was Magnus Brucker, an immigrant from Germany who studied medicine at the universities at Heidelberg and Strasburg. He came to the United States in 1848, settling in Troy, Indiana. He was elected to the House of Representatives as a Republican in 1860 before the Civil War and again in 1866. Brucker enlisted in 1862 in the Indiana 23rd Volunteer Regiment and was commissioned as an assistant surgeon, soon being promoted to surgeon in September of that year despite wishing to resign as early as June 1862.

Brucker must have noticed that Lucy had skills beyond those of a cook and laundress that could be useful to him as a surgeon in the regimental hospital. Better yet, perhaps Lucy advocated for herself, insisting on a better station within the ranks. The need was great, after all. At the beginning of the Civil War, there were only eighty-six men serving as surgeons or assistant surgeons in the Union with a budget of $90,000 in 1860. By the end of the Civil War, that had ballooned 12,000 surgeons and a budget of more than $47,000,000.

Brucker unofficially appointed Lucy to the position of regimental nurse in 1862, shortly after she joined the troops in Bolivar. He promised her she would eventually be paid in exchange for her service. Similar but inconsistent promises of payment for labor were made to Black men and women across all the refugee camps. As Lucy would find out, she would never receive the payment she was promised. Records show she was not alone. For example, Nancy Jones, a washerwoman and cook under the supervision of a surgeon at Hygeia Hospital, was promised pay for her service. When she quit after six months, she was given a paltry twenty-five cents as a gift. It was within Brucker's purview as the surgeon to appoint his nurses, though Lucy found out nearly thirty years later that this verbal contract, made on honor alone, would not withstand

Outdoor scene of two women nursing wounded and sick Union soldiers, 186[?].
Wood Engraving, U.S. National Library of Medicine. Images from the History of
Medicine. http://resource.nlm.nih.gov/101437576.

the scrutiny of laws that prohibited both females and Black people from
serving as nurses in an official capacity.

In the early years of the Civil War, volunteer regiments were especially prone to disease because the conditions of camps were deplorable.
The public outcry over conditions reached such a fever pitch that the
Sanitary Commission was established to oversee the needs of volunteer
regiments. The chaotic and inconsistent method of recruiting to fill
doctor positions through the Sanitary Commission differed from state
to state, stymying progress. The abilities and qualifications of appointed
surgeons varied greatly. Most had never treated a gunshot wound. Some
were uncertified, while others were alcoholics or downright negligent of
their posts and patients.

Despite the disparate quality of appointed doctors, Brucker was, by all accounts, an "able and efficient" surgeon. Colonel William L. Sanderson, in a report from the field in Pittsburgh in March 1862, expressed his gratitude for Brucker's "kind and successful treatment of [the] wounded upon the field and at the hospital." Brucker served in that capacity until the end of the war in 1865. Brucker was an ardent and open opponent of slavery. His abolitionist stance was rooted in both moral and political grounds. He abhorred the "damnable institution" of slavery but was also concerned about the free labor economy. Brucker had hoped to avoid the Civil War and that slavery would simply "pass in time" because it was "incompatible with a free Republic," but, alas, war was a necessity. In an 1864 letter written to his wife from the battlefield in Atlanta, Georgia, he passionately wrote what he called an "epistle" about the long-waging war:

> Slavery in all parts of the United States must be forbidden, to end any further conflict, and to open this country for free labor, and to keep it free for our children and children's children. This alone will sanctify the war, and this goal we shall reach, and within the foreseeable future, and even if thousands should still die for the preservation of the Union, the Army will fight in spite of traitors at home, it owes it to its slain and mutilated comrades, who fought for the cause, should we stop halfway now and make a dishonorable peace, which may only last a short time, then we would disgrace thousands.

Not everyone in the regiment felt so strongly about slavery or Union causes as Brucker. The Indiana 23rd Regiment was populated by soldiers largely from the southern border counties of Indiana along the Ohio River, including Floyd, Clark, Harrison, and Crawford, with some from Washington County and a few Kentuckians from across the water. Situated at the physical boundary between North and South along the Ohio River, many of the men who enlisted made their livelihoods in river life. Many of the soldiers were inclined to at least passively accept, if not outrightly support, southern doctrine. What drove many of them to enlist despite their doubts was a common desire to see the Union preserved as a single country.

Men from southern Indiana and Louisville, Kentucky, occupied contentious territory at the boundary of North and South—a "free" state and a slave state—along the Ohio River banks. Many men who might have been sympathetic to one cause or another might have been swayed by loyalties, persuasion, coercion, and pragmatism to fight for the side that they did not fully support. Given their proximities, families and friends contended with each other across enemy lines.

Brucker worked alongside Lucy for at least two years. Surgeons generally disliked working with female nurses because they were not privates subject to military discipline. But working with formerly enslaved women must have given them the right to control their actions differently. Her loyal service and skills must have reinforced his views on the institution of slavery.

As his nurse, Lucy's job would have gotten infinitely more complex. A surgeon's nurse needed to be tireless, industrious, and steadfast. Lucy waited on the fray of battle, ready to race to the side of wounded soldiers. Anna Morris Holstein, who documented her time as a field nurse over three years, describes the selflessness required of nurses on the front:

> It was impossible to be an idler while this gigantic struggle was in progress. The current of swiftly passing events had, all unconsciously, drifted me to this point; I yielded to its force, and commenced this additional labor as part of the work which came unsought. There was not the least recognition of self in any part of it; had there been, or would have been impossible to have gone on with it.

Holstein describes the feeling of being swept up in the machinery of war and how women found themselves compelled to serve. Holstein, an affluent white woman married to a soldier, however, did not have the added consideration of her child like Lucy or her freedom.

Lucy's kind attention to the soldiers was recalled in a newspaper article from 1889 in Wisconsin: "Her hand often lifted the canteen full of water to the lips of the wounded, her ear received the last message of the dying, and the soldiers looked upon her in the light of a friend. She shared their hardships and never grumbled, and in their triumphs she was among the happiest." She sewed buttons, fixed treats, and foraged. Her ability to multitask and meet the needs of the individual soldier was described: "To the lips of one sufferer she would place a cup of milk, at another cot she would pause and bathe a feverish forehead, leaving a cooling cloth as she hurried away, while for another soldier there would be a bowl of appetizing broth. How she managed to secure these delicacies no one cared to ask." The article attributed her ability to forage for the needs of the soldier back to her time as a bonded woman living on a plantation, finding a spring chicken, bowl of milk, or basket of eggs on a "foraging tour."

General Shadrach Hooper described Lucy's bravery and service with great flair and tenderness in a news article many years later: "Even as Jean d'Arc loved the sound of battle, this faithful colored woman drew back the wounded and dying and comforting them in their last hours unmindful of the hail of bullets and crash of artillery." If they could be saved, she pulled them from the field to the regimental hospital for treatment and lovingly nursed them back to health. Some accounts of her life even claim she was "not averse to seizing a rifle and doing effective work against the enemy, but her greatest heroism was fearlessly going to the front to seek out wounded soldiers and officers, all equal in her mind, and administer water to thirsty mouths, pull away wounded soldiers, and gently care for them. She witnessed men gasping their last breaths, whispering comforts to them as their 'angel of mercy.'"

Regimental hospitals were set up some distance from the front line, and this is where the surgeon would await the arrival of patients for procedures. The Civil War was a particularly brutal war. The assistant surgeons and, sometimes, nurses would be closer to the front line. The low-velocity rifles and particular bullets used were more likely to fatally wound a soldier. If they survived, they would battle disease and infection because there was poor understanding of germ theory. Once they arrived at the regimental hospital, the assistant surgeon would remove any debris from a wound, pack it, and dress it to be cared for by the surgeon. Anything could serve as shelter from the weather for surgeries, such as barns, tents, and churches. Wounded men, usually with wounds to their extremities because core bodily wounds were fatal, waited in droves to receive their procedures, often amputations. In addition to the wounded who struggled to fight off infection, soldiers battled bouts of diarrhea, dysentery, and fever. Disease ultimately killed more soldiers than bullets or shells. Lice, mosquitos, and flies spread diarrhea and malaria, and contaminated water supplies spread typhoid. Poor hygiene and insufficiently nutritious or bountiful rations contributed to the spread of disease. Amidst the wounds and illness, Lucy was there to aid in any way possible.

Beyond caring for their wounds and illnesses, Lucy offered soldiers small creature comforts that eased their troubled minds and homesick hearts. Having disposed of many frivolous possessions and lacking many comforts of home, the men of the regiment often bitterly complained about a lack of access to newspapers and letters from home. Lucy offered them some consoling as they mended and yearned for news from home. Documentation shows that some soldiers in hospitals wanted to address their nurses, white or Black, with titles less formal than madam or even nurse, so they added domestic and familial nicknames, such as Mother. Lucy was affectionately called Aunt Lucy by the soldiers of the Indiana 23rd Regiment, a moniker that would follow her for decades after the war's end.

Caring for all the soldiers, regardless of rank, was important to Lucy, but she also had to navigate a complex class hierarchy to maintain her position. While surgeon Brucker did receive accolades for his great service, it is possible he also leveraged his high position within the ranks for personal benefit. In September 1864, Colonel B. F. Potts of the 32nd Ohio Volunteers, 1st Brigade, 4th Division, wrote a damning letter that accuses Brucker of neglect of duty. He claims that Brucker and another medical officer in the 53rd Illinois Volunteers were "scarcely ever to be found when wounded and sick required attention." More egregiously, he asserts they used an ambulance to transport their private baggage, leaving sick and disabled soldiers "to the mercy of the enemy." Nurses, especially Black nurses, had little recourse if they witnessed abuse of privileges. Accounts from other nurses on the front, such as those of Sophronia Bucklin's recollections "In Hospital and Camp," indicate that nurses had to navigate a very risky line between strictly obeying doctors' orders and willingly disobeying in service of the soldiers. If the accusations against

Brucker were true, it's likely that nurse Lucy would have stepped in to fill the void, caring for the neglected soldiers as best she could in the doctor's absence.

Regardless of the complex social, gender, and racial hierarchies, Lucy was committed; she stayed with the Indiana 23rd Regiment throughout the war, traveling to twenty-eight battle sites and camps across the Southeast. Although the Indiana 23rd engaged in skirmishes with Confederate cavalry while stationed in Bolivar, the first real taste of wartime battle for Lucy must have been on August 30 in nearby Purdy, just a couple months after joining them. It was also probably her first opportunity to demonstrate her ability to contribute more than cooking and laundering. Perhaps Lucy watched from a safe distance as men were brought back to camp, and she stood ready to dress wounds or lift water to their lips. She offered comfort, care, and companionship as those soldiers healed.

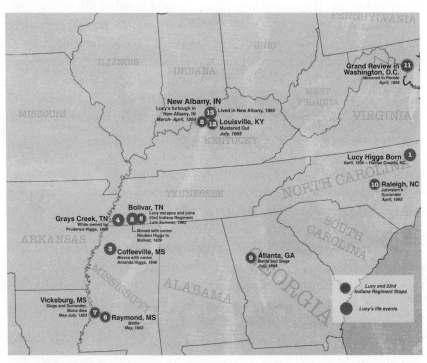

Map of sites of Lucy's life events and select battles of the Indiana 23rd Regiment in the Civil War.

Her care for them must have been sincere and deep because the soldiers would remember her with great tenderness for decades after the war.

Life and Loss on the Front

In the fall of 1862, the Indiana 23rd Regiment went to battles in Corinth and Matamora, then marched from Bolivar, Tennessee, to the Hatchee River on October 5. Then they took on an arduous march—fifty-two miles in two days—in pursuit of Ripley and another in November to join General Grant's central Mississippi campaign toward Vicksburg. This mission was foiled; Van Dorn captured Holly Springs and destroyed supplies, forcing abandonment of the expedition.

In the midst of this march, Lucy traversed potentially familiar territories very close to her former residence in Coffeeville, Mississippi, where she resided for a short time. Although Lucy had moved several times in her life, this caravan and the relentless travel of life on the front was taxing to say the least. While regiments were judged or remembered by the casualties, what defined a regiment most was the time it spent marching. The Indiana 23rd campaigned for 1,400 days but saw battle only on fourteen days and a siege of 123 days. So marching took up more than 1,000 days of their service. A regiment generally traveled with the infantry, artillery, and cavalry units, supported by miles of wagons loaded with food, medical supplies, and ammunition. Marches may be as long as twenty-five miles a day for many days in a row. They would cross waist-deep streams where wagons would get mired in mud and endured severe winter conditions. Lucy usually followed the caravan on foot, carrying Mona across her shoulders, singing lullabies and river songs to soothe the child on the long journeys. Once the men got to know and admire Lucy, they would pick her up on the wagon train. The men would lovingly croon to the little girl to earn her giggles and glee.

Their command reached the Yoknapatawpha River in Mississippi on Christmas Eve 1862. The entire command, especially the Indiana 23rd, was desperately low on rations. For nearly ten days, they relied on the benevolence of people in a Confederate region where two other armies had already marched. Lucy was a formerly enslaved woman with her young child traveling on foot in the cold winter months relying on the willingness of strangers (most of whom probably did not believe in your right to freedom or actively fought against the Union) to provide nourishment for her family's survival. Undoubtedly, soldiers got the best of the rations, which, despite no longer being enslaved, Lucy probably had to prepare for them. That Christmas, they ate dry corn ground into a meal or popped in the fire. Or they ate the field beans grown primarily for slave hands and given the unsavory name of "nigger" beans by the soldiers. Were Lucy and her fellow contraband of war forced to pick those beans? Prepare them? Hear the slurs from the soldiers' mouths as they asked for their helping? Lucy had to have a resolve to set aside these discrepancies, serve with purpose, and build lifelong relationships with the men and women of the regiment despite the subtle and not-so-subtle offenses.

Finally, the railroad was repaired, and some supplies reached the troops. In January 1863, they were asked once again to march, this time to Colliersville, Tennessee, where heavy snows made roads impassable.

Lieutenant William P. Davis of the Indiana 23rd Regiment at age eighteen before the Civil War, ca. 1853. Courtesy of the Floyd County Library, New Albany, Indiana.

Weary and worn, they marched again to Memphis but not at full strength. Many soldiers had to travel by train because of exhaustion and lack of food or shoes. Yet they were encouraged by the promise of rest as they prepared for their most significant campaign yet: Vicksburg.

In Memphis, the troop regained strength and were newly equipped. They embarked on a steamer on February 21 headed toward Lake Providence, Louisiana, where General Grant, in command of Union forces, was gathering his army for a full assault on Vicksburg, the final stronghold of the Confederacy. Colonel Sanderson was detached from the regiment and stayed in Memphis, and Lieutenant William P. Davis assumed command of the regiment.

Three years into the Civil War, while the regiment prepared for Vicksburg, the date January 1, 1863, marked the debut of the Emancipation Proclamation, which declared "that all persons held as slaves" within the rebellious states "are, and henceforward shall be free." While the proclamation was very limited—excluding, for example, the critical border states and secessionist states in northern control—it was a symbolic declaration that made each subsequent victory of the Union army a victory toward freedom.

The Emancipation Proclamation also officially sanctioned the enlistment of Black soldiers in the army—the United States Colored Troops (USCT). While they had long wanted to enlist, laws dating back to 1792 prohibited their enlistment. Lincoln had been an advocate for enlistment well before 1862, but he was again concerned about losing the border states of Kentucky, Missouri, Maryland, and Delaware, effectively turning 50,000 soldiers against the Union. Also, there were strong beliefs, even among Union supporters, that Black men were inferior to white men and could not serve as soldiers. Employing Black men as anything more than laborers was believed to demoralize the white soldier. General Nathaniel P. Banks issued a General Order in 1863 that declared the enlistment of Black troops a matter not of equality but of necessity. Black men should be enlisted to help in any way possible, especially because the cause was as near to him as any other man. Ultimately, however, when it finally became a matter of life or death that a Black body could take a bullet as well as a white body, sentiment began to shift. Once Black troops could prove their mettle in battle, many Union soldiers changed their attitudes.

The service of enlisted Black troops *and* the informal work of formerly enslaved refugees were critical in the capture of Vicksburg, the final stronghold of the Confederacy. The USCT participated in the campaign and siege of Vicksburg during the Battle of Milliken's Bend, Louisiana, and Goodrich's Landing, Louisiana. Their battles were brutal, as described by William Lloyd Garrison in the *Liberator*: "Upon both sides, men were killed with the butts of muskets. White and black men were lying side by side, pierced by bayonets, and in some instances, transfixed to the earth. In one instance, two men—one white and one black—were found dead, side by side, each having the other's bayonet through his body." The struggle "was a contest between enraged men; on the one side from hatred of race and on the other, desire for self preservation, revenge for past grievances, and the inhuman murder of their comrades."

Thousands of African Americans were sent to work on the canal being constructed in Vicksburg, which would change the course of the river, and its success would give advantage that was "beyond computation" by opening Port Hudson to the Mississippi. The construction of the canal was said to be able to "save a battle." Because he could not provide provisions for refugee women and children who were starving, General Grant also employed Black women and children to work the abandoned plantation fields. Add to this the service of cooks, laundresses, and unofficial nurses such as Lucy, and the contributions and sacrifices African Americans made toward freedom are evident. Unfortunately, however, the effort failed. Grant had to rethink his approach to Vicksburg, leading to the land campaign and the multiple battles in Mississippi in which the 23rd Indiana fought with Lucy as nurse.

The Indiana 23rd Regiment did their part in the campaign at Vicksburg. Composed mostly of steamboat men, they were called to man the steamers *J. W. Cheeseman* and *Horizon*. They experienced assault from enemy lines as steamers provided little shield. Between April 25 and 30, they marched from Miliken's Bend to near Grand Gulf and fought in Port Gibson on April 30. More battles ensued, as did losses of life at Thompson Hill and Bayou Pierre. On May 12, they reached Raymond,

This print, published by the Supervisory Committee for Recruiting Colored Regiments, served as a recruitment poster for the USCT. P. S. Duval & Son Lith, *Come and Join Us Brothers*, 1863–1865. Chromolithograph. Harry T. Peters, "America on Stone." Lithography Collection, National Museum of American History.

The refugee men in this image were protected from return to their enslavers as contraband of war under the Confiscation Act of 1861. James F. Gibson, photographer. *A Group of "Contrabands,"* Virginia, 1862 [Hartford, CT: The War Photograph & Exhibition Co., No. 21 Linden Place]. Photograph. https://www.loc.gov/item /2011660086.

about thirty miles from the stronghold in Vicksburg. In that skirmish, they took a significant hit, with 127 men killed, wounded, or missing. It was the worst battle of the Indiana 23rd's Vicksburg campaign. According to the recollections of regiment historian Shadrach Hooper,

Cutting the canal opposite Vicksburg. Sketched by Mr. Theodore R. Davis, Vicksburg, Mississippi, 1862. Photograph. https://www.loc.gov/item/2008680156.

The regiment, having become detached from the main body, had marched into what was practically an ambush and alone met the onslaught of five Confederate regiments . . . being almost entirely surrounded . . . they successfully emerged from what seemed to be an almost hopeless position, fell back to the main line, re-formed, and continued in the engagement.

They fought through the night, overtaking the enemy on the morning of May 14 in an open-field battle with comparably few casualties. They continued the march toward and engaged in small skirmishes along the route to Vicksburg. They ended up taking a forty-day-long position, alongside the Illinois 45th, at the base of the enemy's works, where General John A. Logan's troops were stationed. During that long stay, in constant threat of enemy attack by hand grenades and shells, the soldiers slept in hillside trenches for shelter.

When the Illinois 45th and Indiana 23rd regiments finally entered into Vicksburg on July 4, they were among the troops designated in a post of honor to enter the city to receive surrender. Lucy was there to witness the occasion and stand proud among the men and women she served with. The Indiana 23rd Regiment remained in Vicksburg on duty through February 1864. During this time, they were tasked with thwarting the last gasps of enemy efforts.

Lucy and Mona had survived the escape from enslavement, endured harsh conditions on the front, avoided injury, witnessed ruined cities, slept in wet camp sites, and weathered meager supply rations. Through Lucy's industrious loyal service and tenacious survival, they could see the prospect of freedom in the Emancipation Proclamation and the siege of Vicksburg. The end that could inspire new beginnings was in sight.

The trenches excavated by Major General John A. Logan's troops during the siege of Vicksburg. In the distance is Shirley House, also known as Wexford Lodge (National Park Service, 2013). *Quarters of Logan's Division in the trenches in front of Vicksburg.* Photographed 1863, printed between 1880 and 1889. https://www.loc.gov/item/2013649023.

Alas, between the surrender in July 1863 and February 1864, when the troops left Vicksburg, young Mona, only about four years old, died from an "exposure incident from camp life." Hopefully, Lucy did not have to watch Mona suffer illness for long. Members of the regiment recalled decades later, "In the siege of Vicksburg, after the city had been captured, our regiment was one of the first to go in and receive surrender and Aunt Lucy followed in our wake. A short time afterward her child died. It almost broke the mother's heart. The men too had grown to be so fond of Mona and it was a sincere pang that went through the entire Twenty-third." Many soldiers from the regiment lined the makeshift grave site, a trench in the hillside above Vicksburg. Major Hooper said there was "an elaborate funeral" for the little girl, where many "silent figures in blue" held the same earth that "covered up a portion of Aunt Lucy's heart." The most common war experience was death, shared between opposing soldiers, ranks, races, genders, and ages.

Lucy probably had the opportunity to prepare Mona's body for a spiritual burial. Knowing that Mona would enjoy the blessings of heaven and a familial reunion untouched by sickness and war would have comforted Lucy in the darkest of times. The prevailing belief in the nineteenth century was in the assured salvation of infants, children, and even older youths.

According to the recollections of Shadrach Hooper years later, Lucy's husband joined the USCT. Calvin (or perhaps George) Higgs was very likely Lucy's husband, had shared a domestic life with Lucy, fathered her child, and escaped enslavement by her side. While it is unclear if Lucy and Calvin shared a domestic relationship of any nature, it seems likely given their many years spent together in bondage. If they did share a union, it is unlikely that they had a marriage in any official capacity that was recognized by the government or the church. They may have had a functional marriage recognized by their slave community. However, it was common for formerly enslaved couples, married or not, to be married while on Union lines in a capacity recognized by the federal government and sanctioned by the church to avoid a sinful concubinage and gain legal protections. In camps across the country, missionaries and military authorities married couples whose relationship was equally true regardless of its official recognition.

Records show that Calvin enlisted in the USCT at the age of twenty-nine on December 1, 1863, in Vicksburg, Mississippi. It is not clear if he enlisted before or after the death of Mona. Perhaps he was compelled to fight in honor of his fallen daughter, unable to bear the burden of her death as a passive bystander of the war effort. Or perhaps he joined prior to her death, and Lucy endured her grief without the comfort of her partner. Regardless of the details of the timing, he served loyally over the years with daily duty as a cook. Lucy and Calvin never reunited, but he did muster out of service on May 20, 1866. Lucy's connections to her past, her friends and family, were lost to the ravages of time and distance, consumed by the history of slavery and war.

SHERMAN'S MARCH TO THE SEA

The Indiana 23rd Regiment remained in Vicksburg until February 3, 1864, when they joined Sherman on his campaign to Meridian, Mississippi. The Indiana 23rd was responsible for destroying a railroad track, crippling the 100-mile supply chain from Jackson to Meridian. Finally, at the end of March 1864, the regiment was granted the requisite thirty-day furlough. Lucy accompanied the men to New Albany. She faced a difficult choice. Would she remain in New Albany and begin to build a new life there in anticipation of the end of the war? Would she now grieve the loss of her child and family? Or would she return to the battlefield with the soldiers? As contraband, she was not obliged to return, though she needed the financial remuneration of which she had been assured. More likely, it was her calling to return to service, her need to actively participate in the battle for her own freedom.

While Lucy had few plausible alternatives, she probably chose to resume her service and accompany the regiment as they entered the last years of battle in the Civil War out of a sense of duty and patriotism. Lucy's loyalty to the regiment was unparalleled. They took off via steamer in May 1864 and joined the siege of Atlanta. Between June and September 1864, they participated in numerous engagements, among them the assaults at Kennesaw Mountain, the Chattahoochee River, and Peach

Tree Creek (where Walter Q. Gresham was seriously wounded) as well as the Battle of Logan's Cross Roads and heavy skirmishes at Utoy Creek. They participated in the advance on Jonesboro and Lovejoy Station and into Alabama under the command of John Bell Hood's notoriously reckless leadership. Between engagements, they occupied the trenches and endured daily constant fire. Indiana 23rd soldiers recollected that Aunt Lucy was not averse to picking up a gun and going directly into battle when called on, but her passion was for caring for the sick and wounded.

The Indiana 23rd followed Hood's command almost to the Tennessee River when they made a right-about to join General William Tecumseh Sherman in Atlanta to prepare for the famed "March to the Sea." The Atlanta campaign aimed to cut off Atlanta's vital supply lines that provided Confederate troops with reinforcements, ammunition, and goods, such as clothes, first-aid medicines, and equipment. As Atlanta lay smoldering, Sherman and his troops began their audacious, infamous March to the Sea, a massive scorched-earth campaign that ended in the port city of Savannah, Georgia, on December 21. Sherman's approach to warfare was relentlessly cruel. In his Special Field Orders No. 120 on November 9, 1864, Sherman authorized a new kind of warfare "should guerrillas or bushwhackers molest our march, or should the inhabitants burn bridges, obstruct roads, or otherwise manifest local hostility, then army commanders should order and enforce a devastation more or less relentless according to the measure of such hostility." In a telegram to Ulysses S. Grant, he wrote, "Until we can repopulate Georgia it is useless to occupy it, but utter destruction of its roads, houses, and people will cripple their military resources . . . I can make the march and make Georgia howl." While Sherman specifies that soldiers "will endeavor to leave with each family a reasonable portion for their maintenance," it was not always judiciously practiced. Stories of the atrocities enacted on civilians in the wake of the March to the Sea are devastating. Civilians, including women and children, were not immune to his vengeful pursuit of victory. Sherman's men cut a path 300 miles long and sixty miles wide as they passed through Georgia, destroying factories, bridges, railroads, and public buildings.

On November 15, 1864, U.S. forces led by Sherman burned nearly all of the captured city of Atlanta. More than 3,000 buildings (including businesses, hospitals, homes, and schools) were destroyed. Along the march, all "able-bodied" Black men and women were taken along to be of service to the troops. Sherman insisted on the expedient organization of a "pioneer battalion" for each army corps that was "composed if possible of Negroes." Pioneer battalions were the pick, ax, and shovel workers that built the roads and bridges for the rest of the army to traverse. While the labor of Black men and women was crucial to the efficacy of the army, Sherman reminded his command that they needed to consider the "question of supplies" when recruiting Black workers because their primary duty was to "see to those who bear arms." In other words, the Black men and women who joined the march would be the last to receive the meager rations and supplies.

The Indiana 23rd was encamped near Atlanta at West Point when the Indiana 23rd Regiment joined Sherman's March on November 15, arriving in Savannah, Georgia, on December 10. Along the march, they were actively engaged in battle at Oconee River and Ogoochee River, two engagements that caused the greatest delays and heaviest fighting encountered during the campaign. Once they arrived in Savannah, they participated in the eleven-day siege. They endured heavy fire each day, though their casualties were minor.

The greatest suffering, however, was from low rations. They lacked provisions and were supposed to forage for supplies in the towns they passed through prior to battle. According to Sherman's grand plan, "The army will forage liberally on the country during the march." Foraging was to be the primary method of obtaining rations to support the efficiency of the march without concern for access to supply lines. They were expected to forage for three days to support ten days of rations. Lucy was known to be an industrious forager, but the pressure must have been incredible on her and her counterparts to adequately sustain and ration the supplies for all Union troops. Supplies did not reach the Indiana 23rd Regiment until the day after the evacuation of Savannah.

They remained in camp around Savannah until the early part of July 1865. They resumed their march for the campaign through the Carolinas

George N. Barnard was the official photographer of the Chief Engineer's Office. Between September and November 1864, Barnard documented Sherman's troops in Atlanta, providing a record of the physical damage the attack rendered on the city. George N. Barnard, photographer. *General William T. Sherman on horseback at Federal Fort No. 7, 1864*. Photograph. https://www.loc.gov/item/2018666970.

George N. Barnard, photographer, Atlanta. *The shell-damaged Ponder House, Atlanta, 1864.* Photograph. https://www.loc.gov/item/2018666976.

and on to Sherman's final battle in Bentonville, North Carolina, on March 19 and 20, 1865. As a troop, the Indiana 23rd had been in Grant's first battle and Sherman's last. Lucy was with them for about thirty of their forty-three engagements over four years. They received news of the fall of Richmond and assisted Sherman's army in the surrender of Johnston's army at Raleigh, North Carolina, on April 26, 1865.

THE CONCLUSION OF WAR

By some accounts, a total of 345 soldiers of the Indiana 23rd Regiment were killed in battle or died of wounds, and another 179 died of disease, a total loss of 524 soldiers. The true toll is undoubtedly greater—people like Mona who became the unnamed and uncounted collateral damage of warfare. Lucy was the longest-serving member of the medical staff of the regiment, in part because she could not be reassigned because she was not officially employed. At some point in their years together, she probably cared for every member of the troop.

Lucy never received payment for her service in the war. Her white male soldier counterparts did receive their payments—albeit often late and partial. She continued working empty-handed. If there weren't enough resources and money to pay the soldiers on roll, what was left for the sustenance and support of the hundreds of contraband in their ranks who worked to build fortifications, feed the soldiers, launder their clothes, and nurse their wounds? The battle for legitimacy and compensation would continue for decades for those women and Black Americans who worked alongside the white Union troops.

While the war brought Lucy opportunity and the prospect of freedom, it also delivered intense personal tragedy. She left behind her siblings, lost her husband to the cause, and watched her beloved child die from conditions in the camp. In contrast to perceptions that enslaved people were passive recipients of freedom bestowed on them by Yankees, Lucy's story, like so many others who served in the war, illustrates the intense self-sacrifice made by Black men and women to attain freedom. They, too, went deep into the war zones, working to survive bloody battles in a brutal Civil War that tore the nation apart to reconcile its brutal past. Lucy's struggle can be linked to the central narrative of agency and natural rights for Black Americans who worked to define, shape, and control their own lives in the context of slavery and white oppression. With the close of the Civil War, Lucy now faced the enormous task of deciding what comes next.

4

FINALLY FREE

THE GRAND REVIEW

The Confederate capital at Richmond, Virginia, fell to Union forces on April 2, 1865, and the Confederates effectively surrendered at Appomattox on April 9, one week later. The nation and world grieved at the news that President Abraham Lincoln had been assassinated by Confederate loyalists on April 14, 1865, less than one week after surrender at Appomattox. President Andrew Johnson took office the following day. Despite the critical victories that would preserve the Union and effectively end the war, the last slaves were not freed until June 19, now commemorated as Juneteenth, when Texas was ordered to comply. The formal declaration by President Andrew Johnson declared "that the said insurrection is at an end and that peace, order, tranquility, and civil authority now exist in and throughout the whole of the United States of America."

After the surrender at Appomattox, the Indiana 23rd Regiment, including Lucy, marched through Richmond and on to Washington, D.C., to join the Grand Review, a military victory parade. President Johnson took the honored seat that would have belonged to Abraham Lincoln in the viewing stands. For two days, May 23–24, 1865, about 150,000 men marched in the Grand Review. For the Indiana 23rd, it

The Grand Review at Washington, D.C., on May 23, 1865. The glorious Army of the Potomac passing the head stand. Lithograph by E. Sachse & Co., Boston. Library of Congress.

was a final promenade on a gorgeous day before being mustered out of service.

The Indiana 23rd was one of the largest regiments of General Grant's army, comparable to the USCT 54th Massachusetts Infantry Regiment with about 1,000 soldiers. Major Shadrach Hooper recalled the occasion:

> Following the surrender, the regiment proceeded north by easy marches through Richmond and on to Washington at which point it participated in the triumphant march of the concentrated armies of the United States through the streets of the capital and past the reviewing stands of the great commanders whose ability and courage had brought to a successful ending the most wicked war that had occurred during the age of civilization; and only the presence of the great guiding mind of the loyal side of the conflict, whose thread of life had been snapped by the hand of an assassin, could have added to the joy and pride of this crowning occasion.

They marched to the U.S. Capitol, proceeding northwest on Pennsylvania Avenue toward the White House. The troops were lined up for maximum theatrical effect, some queuing up as early as 2:00 a.m. to ensure that the twenty-five-mile-long column of soldiers would be able to pass the presidential viewing stand. They were instructed to keep the column moving at all costs—no cheering or stopping. The sheer size of the parade had never before occurred on American soil. In no previous American war had there been a gathering of soldiers en masse at the conclusion of battle.

While Lucy marched with the Indiana 23rd Volunteer Regiment to and perhaps in the Grand Review, none of the 18,000 members of the USCT participated in the parade. In fact, many had served longer than the regiments that marched in the parade. The few Black members of the parade were used as comic relief or to entertain the spectators in a most appalling manner. Some marched as part of noncombat "pick-and-shovel" labor brigades. Others marched alongside soldiers as contraband of war in the literal sense, with other "spoils of war" carried by mules. Two large Black soldiers from Sherman's troops rode small mules, their feet dragging the ground. Whether that was intentional exclusion or a practical

Matthew Brady, *Grand Review of the Great Veteran Armies of Grant and Sherman at Washington, on the 23d and 24th May. Sherman's Grand Army, Looking Up Pennsylvania Avenue from the Treasury Buildings, during the Passage of the "Red Star" Division,* Washington, DC, 1865. New York: E. & H. T. Anthony & Co., American and Foreign Stereoscopic Emporium, 501 Broadway, May. Photograph. https://www.loc.gov/item/2011661094.

condition of their ongoing enlistment duties remains a point of contention among historians, but the omission seems conspicuously intentional. For the tens of thousands of Black Americans who lived and worked in Washington, D.C., and the many more who followed the troops as they marched into the city, the parade must have been symbolic of the tough Reconstruction road ahead. Recognizing the injustice of the exclusion of the USCT, some subsequent marches were organized on a regional level. For example, Black regiments from Pennsylvania and Massachusetts gathered in Harrisburg, Pennsylvania, on November 14, 1865, for their own Grand Review.

Military victory parades had a long history dating back to ancient wars, and the Grand Review had many characteristics of those parades. Ancient texts where such parades were described were popular in antebellum America, as was a vision of the more pure ancient political past, such as the Roman Republic. Furthermore, educated northerners saw the victory parade as symbolic of American exceptionalism, a nationalistic

African American soldiers did not participate in the parade, but some marched for comic relief and the entertainment of the crowds. Their illustration in Frank Leslie's paper exhibits stereotypical characteristics. *The bummers and foragers of Sherman's Army marching in the Grand Review, Washington D.C., May 24, 1865, artist's impression,* from *Frank Leslie's Illustrated Newspaper,* June 10, 1865, 180. House Divided: The Civil War Research Engine at Dickinson College. https://hd.housedivided.dickinson.edu/node/44010.

view of the supremacy of democratic republicanism in America. In other words, American democracy did not fall to civil conflict. The parade was a symbol of America's (white) future. Indeed, four future presidents were Union soldiers and marched in that parade. It was the largest military parade in the history of America to that point.

But Lucy would not have known the classical context of military parades, having never attended formal schooling. And she would not have experienced the parade in the same way that her fellow soldiers or hundreds of thousands of onlookers might have. Lucy probably experienced a surge of pride in her service. Her heart was weighted, however, by the loss of her daughter some short months before. She could have felt incredible optimism at the prospect of freedom and simultaneously worry that what she would endure in the future would present challenges unknown. But surely, she wanted to see the parade commemorate the most important of issues in her mind and heart: the emancipation of about 4 million enslaved people.

The parade, unfortunately, lacked critical recognition of emancipation or the cost of lives lost in preserving the Union. In harkening back to military victory parades of the past, the celebration emphasized the preservation of the Union, not emancipation. It was not until 1892 and 1915, during reenactment of the Grand Review, that the USCT were allowed to participate. Even then, the emphasis was not on emancipation but on unity. The sentiment was that the USCT deserved equal recognition, but the memorialization was focused on preserving the Union.

Nor was the Grand Review parade of 1865 a memorial to fallen soldiers despite inconceivable casualties after more than four years of Civil War: between 600,000 and 750,000 lives were lost. It was not until 1868 that Memorial Day was inaugurated by the commander in chief, General John A. Logan of the Grand Army of the Republic (GAR), to commemorate the Union dead.

Instead, the white citizen-soldier and the preservation of the Union were the focal points of the parade, not generals. They beamed with pride at the regimental and battle flags. Far from pristine, the banners bore the physical wear and tear of battle, a metaphor for combat and sacrifice. According to all contemporary accounts, the event was unparalleled on

American soil, a true spectacle befitting a momentous occasion even if it did not represent all of those who made sacrifices on behalf of the country.

THE OPPORTUNITY TO CHOOSE

Having endured enslavement, survived the Civil War, and celebrated victory in the Grand Review, Lucy finally had the opportunity to choose what came next: to exert some control over her own destiny. She was no longer bound to the Higgs family or even the Indiana 23rd Regiment. She was faced with a decision: where would she go if she had no home, no work, no family, and a precarious new freedom? She could return to Tennessee and seek the assistance of the Freedman's Bureau; stay in Washington, D.C., with the 40,000 other refugees who remained in the city to work and live in settlements established in abandoned forts; or entrust her freedom to the men of the Indiana 23rd Regiment who encouraged her to return with them to their hometown of New Albany, Indiana. Would she set out to find her remaining relatives? Or would she compartmentalize her grief, hoist her resolve, and move forward to begin a new life?

In the months and years after the Emancipation Proclamation, public sentiment toward freedmen and freedwomen, as well as the federal policies that sought to give them equality, was mixed. Many Black men and women experienced violence in the streets and at the hands of their employers, and their course of action to address these incidents was limited by an overburdened court system that did not have the time, interest, or precedent to deal with such cases. In the wake of the war, the contraband policies that served as a satisfactory stall tactic no longer served the thousands of now free Black men and women who had previously been bound to labor as property. This was no longer a consideration of enslavement but of race. One solution, supported by Lincoln long before emancipation, was to recolonize all the formerly enslaved and Black Americans to another place entirely. Lincoln proposed locations in Central America, Africa, and the Caribbean. After a failed experiment in Haiti, Lincoln abandoned this plan. Stateside attempts to provide work and land for cotton farming were thwarted by angry mobs. Even seemingly supportive

Thomas Nast's celebration of emancipation of southern slaves with the end of the Civil War brings into contrast the life of an enslaved person in the South in comparison to a promising and optimistic future for the free Black people in the United States. Thomas Nast, *Emancipation* (Philadelphia: S. Bott, 1865). Wood engraving. Prints and Photographs Division, Library of Congress. Reproduction number LC-USZ62-2573 (5–9).

abolitionist governors from the North were reluctant to accept migrant African Americans seeking to begin their free lives. Some did find placement in the armed services, but that option was also limited.

The Bureau of Refugees, Freedmen, and Abandoned Lands, or the Freedmen's Bureau, was established by Congress on March 3, 1865, despite Lincoln's initial opposition. The bureau was akin to a welfare agency that was intended to help the transition from enslavement to freedom in the southern states. Local Freedmen's Bureau agents were responsible for implementing federal law but also at odds with resistance of their local population. Some southern whites feared federal regulation, while others believed the assistance allowed for freedmen and freedwomen to live off their dime. But the bureau did great work in the face of nearly insurmountable obstacles and corruption, including feeding the poor, operating hospitals, helping freed people gain labor contracts, and fighting for access to education. They also helped to legalize marriages done during the war and aided with reuniting families separated during the war.

If Lucy returned to Tennessee, she might have received some assistance from the bureau. She could have gone back to the farms from which she escaped to work for a wage as a tenant farmer or domestic servant. Or she could have opted to stay in Washington, D.C., where tens of thousands of contraband refugees had been receiving meager payment for their labors to build fortifications. Those fortifications later housed freed people between 1865 and 1866. Freed people also erected settlements in and near Washington. including Anacostia, Fort Greble, and Freedman's Village in Arlington, Virginia. Washington had already abolished slavery in the capital with the DC Emancipation Act of 1862, nine months prior to the Emancipation Proclamation of 1863, so they had a jump start on postwar reconstruction efforts.

Ultimately, Lucy chose to follow the men of the regiment back to New Albany, Indiana. She had built strong relationships with the veterans, and they had endured unimaginable obstacles and trauma together. They were the closest thing she had to family. Arriving in New Albany was a return to home for the soldiers, but it was totally foreign to Lucy. She had to start from scratch to find a place to live and work to support herself. She would come to rely on that bond with the soldiers to find employment.

The service of most Black cooks, laundresses, and even nurses was forgotten over the years as they struggled to find work that sustained them during the Reconstruction years. Rarely did they have the time or the education to be able to document their service in memoirs, and their official records are sparse. Most formerly enslaved women who served with the Union went into domestic service positions, though a few leveraged their wartime work into postwar success. Susie King Taylor, for example, went on to establish a school to educate freedmen and freedwomen. The nursing profession experienced a surge of professionalization after the Civil War, but few Civil War nurses pursued the path. Nurses' schools that were created postwar did not offer Black women the option to take up nursing. Established on the model of Florence Nightingale's

English schools, America's nursing system had restrictive admission standards that once again disenfranchised working-class women, especially former slaves. The schools admitted only young, white middle-class women. For Lucy, the unappealing choices and restrictions of her race, gender, and status compelled her to follow the soldiers once more to their homes in New Albany, Indiana.

SERVING THE GRESHAMS

Like many other formerly enslaved women during Reconstruction, Lucy's options for employment were limited to some form of domestic labor in the home of a white person. The prospect promised long days of labor with minimal pay and harsh treatment. However, Lucy was fortunate enough to work as a servant in the homes of officers in the Indiana 23rd Regiment, including Major Shadrach Hooper, who had grown to respect and value her. After several years in his home, she went to his neighbors, Walter Quintin Gresham and his wife Matilda, the same Greshams with whom Lucy served in the war. Lucy probably nursed General Gresham back to health when he was badly wounded. By this time, W. Q. Gresham was a rising political star with deep ties to Indiana politics and a close friend of General Grant, and he eventually became U.S. secretary of state in 1893. Lucy claimed to have met many influential political figures throughout her life, and it may have been her connection with the Greshams that gave her that access.

Lucy maintained a close relationship with the Greshams long after her service in their home. Around 1889, Lucy was invited to and attended the very prestigious Chicago wedding of the Greshams' daughter Katie. Once she left for Chicago, she telegraphed General Gresham and was escorted to the event by carriage by Otto Gresham, Secretary Gresham's son and brother to the bride. She was entertained at the lavish Palmer Hotel. Going to Chicago for a full week as an honored guest of the Gresham family must have been an awe-inspiring experience. The Palmer House was the most extravagant hotel in Chicago, perhaps unlike anything Lucy had witnessed in her life. It was still relatively new, built in 1870 and rebuilt in 1873 after a fire, and ornately filled with rare mosaics and Italian marble. It had a grand lobby that evoked English drawing

This is the lavish Palmer House hotel in Chicago, Illinois, where Lucy attended the wedding of General W. Q. Gresham's daughter. Detroit Publishing Co., copyright claimant and publisher (between 1900 and 1910). Photograph. https://www.loc.gov/item/2016813807.

rooms and the lovely Empire Dining Room. As an honored guest at the wedding, Lucy must have been in close proximity to many powerful men who might have been influential in the approval of her controversial pension request years later.

Post-Civil War New Albany

By 1863, New Albany, Indiana, was the second-largest city in Indiana. It had been deeply connected to war efforts, functioning largely as a hospital town with more than twelve hospitals. Every person in the town had been affected, whether as a volunteer caring for the wounded, a pastor asked to help take up collections, or a citizen compelled to give. The loosely organized network of welfare begun by volunteer organizations during the war helped establish long-term care and the beginning of

This painting is a view of New Albany from Silver Hills in 1853, about twelve years prior to Lucy's arrival, by notable New Albany artist George Morrison. Collection of the Cultural Arts Center, Floyd County Library, New Albany, Indiana.

modern welfare services both in New Albany and across the nation. Schools and businesses had been transformed into eleven different hospitals, including public school Upper City School, Lower Market Street School, and Lower Spring Street School, along with the Asbury Female College, Anderson College, and the Female College on Elm Street. Businesses were also transformed into hospitals, such as Scott and Brindley Furniture, the Baltic Saloon, and Woodward Hall, all in downtown New Albany. A hospital boat along the Ohio provided a steady stream of wounded soldiers. The fairgrounds became Camp Floyd (later Camp Noble), where soldiers were trained. Quartermaster depots, arsenals, and barracks all operated out of New Albany. The train depot distributed supplies and ferried soldiers from battle to furlough. Local businesses and industry profited from the war.

New Albany's entire identity was tied to the Civil War and its position along the infamous Mason–Dixon Line. While Lucy was welcomed, not all refugees and migrating free people were equally embraced by the community. Newspaper accounts show the conflict and fanned the flames, making the transition to freedom more challenging for all. John B. Norman, editor of the *New Albany Daily Ledger*, wrote in 1865, "The influx of the 'colored population' into our city continues. Kentucky is rapidly getting rid of a population which has heretofore been productive, and Indiana is adding daily to a population which will prove a public expense." The social, religious, and political ideologies surrounding issues of race in New Albany were complex, influencing the cultural milieu into which Lucy was entering in post–Civil War New Albany. Antebellum and Civil War–era New Albany was a hotbed of pro-Union, anti-slavery, and anti-Black sentiments. Its position as a free state on the Ohio River, the boundary between free territory and slave territory, made it an appealing destination for freedom seekers who were escaping along what was eventually coined the Underground Railroad en route to Canada.

Indiana was admitted to the Union in 1816 as a free state, barring slavery and indentured servitude. However, the state constitution of 1816 did not protect the civil rights of the free Black population. The 1851 state constitution enacted restrictions that prohibited African Americans from migrating to the state and denied Black suffrage to those already residing in the state. They also could not serve in the militia, have interracial marriage, or testify against whites in court. Segregated schools were required in 1869. Some of these laws were established and upheld during the era of "Jim Crow laws," or Black Codes—laws that were established after the Civil War by individual states to deliberately undermine the status of free Black Americans. The social and political hierarchy of whites in Indiana and across the nation was threatened by emancipation and the growth of the Black population in their states, and many residents of the state resisted the erosion of their ways of life. Lucy was witness to and experienced many of the laws that inhibited her freedoms and the freedoms of her fellow Black citizens in New Albany.

On a broader scale, President Rutherford B. Hayes ended Reconstruction in 1877 and pulled U.S. troops, who were providing nominal protections for Black citizens, out of the South. In addition to the formal end of Reconstruction-era policies, there were new laws enacted that disenfranchised tenant farmers who had to rely on the southern landed property owner to divide crop proceeds between himself and lessees and systematic regulation of the voting process that gave considerable power to Democratic politicians to determine voting eligibility. There was a mass exodus of southern Black people to the western and midwestern states, including Indiana, fleeing oppressive policies and growing Klan violence in the South in search of greater opportunity. In Indiana, all of the seven urban centers, including New Albany, experienced significant growth in the Black population, undoubtedly of newly free southern Black Americans looking for better circumstances in the northern states presumed to be more sympathetic and aligned to their cause. New Albany experienced a 90 percent growth in the Black population between 1860 and 1870 alone. The growth of the Black population across Indiana was consistently higher than that of the white population in the decades after the Civil War. John H. Clay, a North Carolina reverend for the African Methodist Episcopal Church, shared pamphlets touting Indiana's "rich state of fertile lands" and a place where "all stand equal before the law—the black man being protected in his contracts, property, and person the same as the white." They compared the mass exodus to the children of Israel marching out of Egypt.

The reality of Indiana's policies toward equality was subtly different from the declarations in the pamphlets. The Indiana Republican State Platform of 1878 endorsed equality "without regard to race, color, condition or occupation" but also added the qualifier that it was against any "exclusive privileges to individuals and classes." This is an indirect way of stating that the party might not support the "special interests" of the Black population or fund any initiatives to support efforts to reach equal status. Ultimately, any promotion of Black migration to Indiana was satisfying the desire to meet the demands of labor shortages for menial tasks.

The ongoing racial tensions after the Civil War also led to violent outbursts against the Black population, who suffered enormously without proper legal protections. Indiana became the state with the seventh-highest rate of non-southern racial terror lynchings, with eighteen separate incidents between 1871 and 1950. Lucy undoubtedly knew of the 1871 lynchings that happened in neighboring Clark County.

George Johnson, Squire Taylor, and Charles Davis, all Black men, were accused and acquitted of killing the Cyprus family. Before they were released, a white mob gathered, torturing Squire Taylor before lynching all three men in an act of vigilante justice. It was not until 2022 that the Indiana Senate officially recognized the innocence of George Johnson, Squire Taylor, and Charles Davis in Senate Resolution 36. The threat of violence loomed over Black people trying to establish life in post–Civil War Indiana.

There was tension, too, with Louisville, Kentucky, just across the river. Downtown Louisville was a major center for the trade of enslaved people. Just before the Civil War, Louisville had a population of about 69,739, including 1,948 free Black people and 4,903 enslaved people. Indiana residents feared retribution under the Fugitive Slave Act of 1850 if they aided the escape of an enslaved person, and slave catchers were active throughout southern Indiana. The issue of slavery was contentious from both ethical and economic standpoints. For many, preservation of the Union was so critical that they would allow the institution of slavery to continue in perpetuity. Much of southern Indiana's economic strength relied on the steamboat industry and the South, which had relied on slavery.

On a daily basis, Lucy experienced a society that functionally separated Black citizens from their white counterparts. The 1875 Civil Rights Act required "that all persons within the jurisdiction of the United States shall be entitled to the full and equal enjoyment of the accommodations, advantages, facilities, and privileges of inns, public conveyances on land or water, theaters, and other places of public amusement; subject only to the conditions and limitations established by law, and applicable alike to citizens of every race and color, regardless of any previous condition of servitude." The bill further forbade the barring of any person from jury service because of race and provided that all lawsuits brought under the new law would be tried in federal, not state, courts.

Responses in Indiana to the Civil Rights Act of 1875 were divisive. One newspaper stated it was unconstitutional because "no law could say men are socially equal." A Fort Wayne paper denounced the effects of the new law, lamenting that, "as if by concerted movement, the negroes have everywhere attempted to reap the new and wonderful benefits conferred by the act. They have besieged the theatres, saloons, hotels, and railroad coaches. They have interposed their sable features in the barber shops under the hallucination that the tonsorial artists therein would embark in wool clipping." In other words, white residents were angry that Black citizens now enjoyed the same rights and privileges to pursue "life, liberty, and happiness" under the new laws.

The challenges to the law were swift. The Supreme Court's Civil Rights Cases of 1883 contended that the federal government's jurisdiction could regulate states, not individuals, so the law did not apply to private persons or corporations, effectively ensuring that the equal protection clause of the Fourteenth Amendment to the U.S. Constitution provided no guarantee against private segregation. In 1896, further cases found "separate but equal" accommodations constitutional.

HOME, HEART, AND SUFFRAGE

Long before Lucy attended the lavish wedding of Kate Gresham, Lucy had one of her own. Lucy had concluded either that her husband from her former life as a slave was dead or that she would never hear from him. An article reported, "What became of her companion in slavery, she does not know, as she has never received any information." She never found out that Calvin Higgs, presumably her husband and the father of her now deceased child Mona, had indeed survived the war. He mustered out on May 20, 1866, mere days before the march of the Grand Review. Like Lucy, he had valiantly served the duration of the war, though, unlike Lucy, he had been paid for some portion of his service. While their marriage had likely been informal and not legally binding, most states had passed laws between 1865 and 1866 recognizing prewar slave marriages and legitimizing the children of those marriages. Without any legal documentation of their marriage and no official record of Lucy's service, Lucy and Calvin never found one another after the Civil War. Having lost her husband and child, not to mention her siblings, Lucy had to rebuild a life and family. Immediately in the aftermath of the Civil War, many southern newspapers were flooded with advertisements from

Alfred R. Waud, *Mustered Out*, Little Rock, Arkansas, April 20, 1865. Drawing. Chinese white on green paper. Published in *Harper's Weekly*, May 19,
1866. Prints and Photographs Division, Library of Congress. Reproduction
number LC-USZ62-175 (5–1).

former slaves seeking out their lost relatives, often naming their enslavers
directly. No such record of Lucy's efforts has yet been discovered.

All former slaves were granted the right to make contracts, including the right to marry, in the Civil Rights Acts of 1866, about one year
after the Emancipation Proclamation. While many veteran abolitionists
believed their work was done at the conclusion of the war, others, such
as Frederick Douglass, wanted to see the repeal of racist laws that were
established prior to the Civil War to oppress free African Americans.
They needed to keep fighting for the repeal of racist laws, for protection
and immunity of citizens, and for Black men's right to vote. The urgency
of the cause was apparent as white southerners resorted to violence and
explicit discriminatory laws to intimidate free Black Americans. When
the Civil Rights Act of 1866 was written, it settled debates about states'
rights to create discriminatory laws by guaranteeing there shall be "no
discrimination in civil rights or immunities among the inhabitants of
any State or Territory of the United States on account of race, color, or

previous condition of slavery," followed by an affirmation that all races and colors had the same right to make contracts, give evidence in court, hold real and personal property, benefit from legal proceedings, and be subject to legal penalties. With the deliberate use of the term "inhabitants," Congress was making a broad-stroke claim that all people should be protected against racial discrimination. Ultimately, the term did not stick, but the sentiment did, and marriage, among other civil rights, was now a protected privilege.

While legally binding marriage was finally a guaranteed civil right for African Americans, it proved to be difficult to obtain. The right to choose whether to marry was an integral part of their new freedom associated with public status, state recognition, exercise of personal freedom, and enjoyment of social rights. But there was a dark side to the new laws. Part of the motivation for granting legal marriage was to encourage Victorian ideals of middle-class married life, including fidelity and male authority in the household. There was a perception of loose sexual mores within the Black community, including both men and women. Free Black women were perceived as too independent, and marriage would allow men to assert their control over women's actions. Now unmarried Black men and women who were cohabitating could be punished. Sexual relations outside of marriage, formerly required of the enslaved from their masters or because their marriages were not legally binding, were now considered criminal in some states. Not all former slaves rushed to legalize their marriages. Two systems coexisted in the post–Civil War era: a formal one with legally recognized marriage and an informal one rooted in the systems established during slavery. Despite these complicating factors, the right to marry was considered an important measure of race progress. In 1868, the Fourteenth Amendment extended citizenship to all persons born in the United States and guaranteed that all citizens were equally protected under law.

Lucy was lucky to find the companionship of John H. Nichols, a Tennessee Civil War veteran of the 8th U.S. Colored Heavy Artillery that enlisted in Paducah, Kentucky. He was probably born in Virginia to Leander and Sena Nichols, and he was one of eight children. His parents and family were free Blacks in Washington County, Tennessee, at least through the census of 1850. John's mother died sometime between 1850 and 1860. His siblings dispersed by 1860, though his eldest sister Sabus Sarah lived with John and his father Leander in Tennessee. Again, their race was marked as "B F," for "Black and Free," in the 1860 census.

The circumstances that drove John and his father to move to Indiana between the end of the Civil War and 1870 are unknown, but it was a fortuitous move for Lucy and John. Leander worked in New Albany as a day laborer, and John was a fireman at the DePauw Glass Works factory in New Albany, one of the largest glass factories in the nation. As New Albany's boat-building trade was waning, the industrial infrastructure to support the glass industry was growing. Coal to feed the fires, manned by Nichols, among others, came from a Pittsburgh barge. Profits from the glass industry promoted the growth of other industrial manufacturing, including an ironworks, a cotton and woolen mill, a hosiery mill, tanneries, and other factories.

On April 13, 1870, Lucy Higgs married John Nichols. In contrast to the unofficial slave marriage that Lucy had with Calvin, John and Lucy were able to make choices about the location, vows, celebration, food, and attendees. The gathering would likely include their kin, close friends, and perhaps employers. It is likely that Leander, John's father, was in attendance because the 1870 census shows that Lucy and John lived together in Leander's home, whose real estate property was valued at $300 (though this may have been a typo because John owned the home). Maybe some of the veterans with whom Lucy had served were in attendance. Lucy and John probably adopted some white customs for the marriage ceremony and celebration, such as carrying flowers and serving cake. Lucy would have lovingly selected a bridal gown, perhaps long and white with a veil, as an opportunity to showcase her physical beauty and moral purity. John set aside his work clothes to get the best suit he could manage. They were able to obtain an official marriage license guaranteeing their legal and God-ordained right to marry. Their marriage ceremony and celebration was a mark of their free status as much as it was a legal and symbolic commitment, especially for Lucy, who could not have had such a commemoration under the ownership of the Higgs family.

Lucy and John were married by Reverend Charles Edwards, the pastor who started the Colored Baptist Church in 1867. In many African American communities, including southern Indiana, life centered around church. The church and its pastor influenced social, political, and economic decisions, and the pastor served as a community leader, teacher, and businessman. Black churches provided the nexus of families and communities to enable and promote civic engagement and political action. For Lucy, the church may have provided her with a community of people who could understand something of her experience as a former slave. According to records and oral history, the following people were congregants at the Second Presbyterian Church and former slaves: Samuel Cook, a man named Homer, Alex Woodsen, Andrew J. and Unity Murphy, Grandison Webb, Elizabeth Kincheloe, the Blakemore family, and William Blake Dawson. It is probable there were other former slaves among the congregants in addition to those Black members who were free prior to emancipation. Perhaps some of these people celebrated with John and Lucy on their wedding day.

The congregants were likely aware of its significant role in New Albany's Black history, particularly during the abolitionist movement and as a site of the Underground Railroad. The location of the current Second Baptist Church began as the Second Presbyterian Church, constructed between 1849 and 1852 and spearheaded by John Bishop and James Brooks, both of whom were known to treat African Americans with dignity and provide services. John Bishop had baptized a Black woman on her deathbed, and Presbyterian ministers were known to perform marriage ceremonies for African Americans. In the 1850s, James Brooks had been the president of the New Albany and Salem Railroad, a verified route for freedom seekers who both traveled in the cars and followed the rails on foot as they headed north. In all of his capacities, it was likely he gave passes to ride the rails legitimately.

The Second Presbyterian Church became the locus of numerous antislavery events between 1850 and Lucy's wedding in 1870. In 1851, John Guest Atterbury, from Detroit, Michigan, was installed as pastor of the Second Presbyterian Church, the same day as the dedication of the new edifice. The church was dedicated on July 31, 1852, and Reverend

Second Baptist Church, New Albany, Indiana, ca. 1892. Courtesy of the Floyd County Library, New Albany, Indiana.

John Guest Atterbury was appointed pastor at that time and served through July 1866. At the invitation of Atterbury, Reverend Henry Little was invited as a guest preacher. Little was a very strong antislavery man who spoke out openly against slavery and indicated a decidedly antislavery sentiment at the church. The church went on to establish a mission in the traditionally Black West Union neighborhood during the Civil War. In 1862, anti-Black riots resulting in several murders of Black citizens broke out in New Albany. Reverend Atterbury gave a sermon that was later published, stating, "Right does not depend on color. God is no respecter of persons or races. He has made all of one blood, and he seeks the good of all and we must seek the good of all within our province." After the passage of the Emancipation Proclamation, famed "conductor" of the Underground Railroad Levi Coffin visited the Second Presbyterian Church to raise money to assist newly liberated slaves. It was not until 1889 that the church was purchased by the Colored Baptist Church, established in 1867, and renamed the Second Baptist Church. Because so many African Americans in the community had close connections to the building there, it was a natural acquisition, and many of the congregants remained with the church.

The church continues today as the Second Baptist Church, nicknamed the Town Clock Church for the prevalent clock that adorned its steeple. It is believed that the steeple was a beacon for fugitives crossing the river before the Civil War. Many of the Black Presbyterian members of the church continued on to join the Second Baptist Church after the purchase. Those members shared an oral history that serves as a record of the Black civil rights activities of the church from before, during, and after the Civil War. The storied past of the church where Lucy and John said their vows probably added another layer of significance to the occasion. Other churches in New Albany share a similar connection to the Underground Railroad, including the Bethel African Methodist Episcopal Church, which was started around 1840 by Bishop Paul Quinn in the West Union neighborhood, where John and Lucy lived.

While the official recognition of marriage was an important development in the rights of Black Americans and one that remained largely intact in the era of Jim Crow laws after 1875, there were other fundamental rights that were gained more slowly. The same year that Lucy and John were married, the Fifteenth Amendment was ratified in 1870, guaranteeing the right to vote for all male citizens. However, that right did not come to Indiana without significant resistance from the Democrats in the legislature. In 1869, seventeen senators and thirty-seven representatives (all Democrats) resigned their seats in an effort to break quorum. After finding some creative loopholes, the General Assembly met and ratified the Fifteenth Amendment in 1870 despite Democratic protests. As a consequence, Republicans lost control of the Indiana General Assembly for the first time since 1860, in large part due to the unpopularity of the amendment. Lucy and John's civil rights were being threatened in the state they chose to call home.

Despite the resistance and challenges, there was also a sense of optimism and hope that prevailed. In an Indianapolis newspaper, Black writer Silas Shucraft wrote a letter to the editor that concludes with this positive outlook on the future of the nation on the occasion of suffrage for the Black man, stating,

> The old *fossils* of the past and the darker eras are fast disappearing, and light, liberal principles, equality and reform are some of the footprints of this age of mighty progression. Old systems and prejudices, engendered by race and color, the more broad, liberal, and philanthropic principles of an enlightened public mind. This car of progres is moving forward and upward, and the puny hands of opposition can not stay its course.

That year proved influential in many ways. Landownership was another crucial part of American identity and a path toward accruing and passing on wealth for recently liberated people. It is important to put that prospect into context. Going back to January 16, 1865, Union general William T. Sherman (of the famed Sherman's March to the Sea) issued Special Field Order No. 15, which called for the redistribution of confiscated southern lands, stating, "The islands from Charleston, south, the abandoned rice fields along the rivers for thirty miles back from the sea, and the country bordering the St. Johns river, Florida, are reserved and set apart for the settlement of the negroes [*sic*] now made free by the acts of war and the proclamation of the President of the United States." This is the order known as "40 Acres and a Mule." Additionally, the communities would be governed by Black leaders, and each family would receive a plot of up to forty acres of tillable land under protection of the military. This revolutionary and daring plan setting aside 400,000 acres was developed between Sherman and twenty Black leaders in Georgia. The meetings were of such enormous consequence and historical significance that the transcripts were presented to Henry Ward Beecher (the famed brother of Harriet Beecher Stowe), read at New York's Plymouth Church, and printed in the *New York Daily Tribune* on February 13, 1865. The response to the order was swift, news spread, and by June of that year, 40,000 freedmen had settled on "Sherman Land." Perhaps Calvin, John, and Lucy had all heard of this promised land. Maybe they had even considered taking their chances after mustering out. Sadly, they would not even have the opportunity because the visionary plan of the order was overturned by Lincoln's successor, Andrew Johnson, who sympathized with the South. All of the land was returned to the original owners. The "40 acres and a mule" promise could have been the first large-scale reparations attempt for newly freed slaves. Despite these early setbacks and increasing segregation and land disputes, ownership of farmland steadily increased in the late 1800s, with an all-time-high national average in 1910. During the Reconstruction period, freed slaves and their descendants accumulated 19 million acres of land.

Between 1870 and 1910, the Black homeownership rate increased by fifteen percentage points, from 8 to 23 percent, one of the largest periods of growth for Black homeownership in the United States. Soon after they married in January 1871, John Nichols became one of those proud homeowners. He bought lots 58 and 59 on Naghel Street, commonly referred to as West Union. He paid $325 to John H. Stotsenburg and his wife Jane. They spent forty years in a home there in the Black neighborhood known as West Union. It was a short carriage ride to downtown New Albany, where they attended church faithfully at Second Presbyterian until Lucy was stricken with paralysis in 1897.

Lucy's home was comfortably furnished, neatly painted, and filled with relics of her service and the relationships she held with the members of her community and the regiment. She had articles of clothing given to her by men of distinction. One of her most prized possessions was a

John and Lucy Nichols lived in this house at 1234 Naghel Street in the historically Black neighborhood of West Union in New Albany, Indiana. Photographs of the home were taken in 1995, and the home has since been demolished. Photographs courtesy of Pamela Peters.

satin circular given to her by General Grant, according to Lucy, in return for a favor she rendered. Perhaps she met him through the Greshams. However, her most cherished possession was a framed photograph of General Gresham and his daughter Katie as a young girl, the same whose wedding Lucy had attended in Chicago. Lucy clearly valued her history and kept mementos to remind her of her service and sacrifices.

While Lucy was widely respected by her community, she also had her share of conflict. In 1884, a woman named Harriet Harper pulled a pistol on Lucy. The circumstances of the altercation are unknown. Harriet was a Black woman, described as "deeply colored," who worked as a laundress. She lived near Lucy in the West Union neighborhood on Walnut Street, just two blocks from Lucy and John's home on Naghel. Lucy appeared before Squire Huckeby to complain that Harper drew a revolver and threatened to shoot her. Harriet first appeared in court on July 28 and was later tried in circuit court on September 13 and acquitted. Harriet must not have remained in New Albany for long because she shows up in only one city directory and no census records from New Albany. Other than conjecture, there is little evidence on which to speculate a cause for this disturbance. Had Harriet, too, endured the hardships of life on a plantation? Did she envy Lucy's status in the community? Did they have a dispute over something more closely related to their homes and neighborhood? Whatever the cause, apparently there was insufficient evidence to form a conviction, and she was acquitted. This neighborhood feud seems to be an anomaly in Lucy's history, and all other evidence indicates she maintained cordial relationships with all members of the community, garnering her the utmost respect.

THE GAR

In addition to her church community, Lucy maintained her relationship with the veterans. While Lucy was never formally acknowledged as enlisted in the Indiana 23rd Regiment because of gender and race, she was considered by the soldiers themselves as a veteran among their ranks. Her honorary position among the soldiers was influenced not only by the quality and longevity of her service but also by the lasting relationships she built.

The veterans acknowledged Lucy's dedication when was made an honorary member of the New Albany, Indiana, Sanderson Post of the Grand Army of the Republic (GAR). While her name does not appear on any official roll, she was touted as a member of the GAR in many local and national public forums and events.

The GAR was a Union veterans' organization formed in April 1866 by Benjamin Franklin Stephenson, a surgeon with the Illinois 14th Regiment, with the intent to form a fraternal brotherhood of veterans. Interest in the organization grew rapidly; there were ten states and the District of Columbia represented at the national encampment in Indianapolis in November 1866. In its early years, however, the organization suffered from a lack of clarity about its mission. The addition of political dimensions in the 1860s and a semi-military restrictive ranking system in the 1870s undermined the growth of the organization and obscured intent. After fizzling out to one mostly Black post in Virginia, the GAR experienced a revival in the 1880s. With heavy recruiting and easing of regulations that made it easier to join and harder to be expelled, membership in the GAR reached its peak in 1890, with more than 400,000 members and 7,000 posts. It was then the largest social and charitable organization in the nation. Almost every prominent veteran was enrolled, including five presidents: Grant, Hayes, Garfield, Harrison, and McKinley.

The GAR had been formed to support fraternity, charity, and loyalty. Fraternity was promoted through regular local meetings, characterized by "campfires," where comrades would gather around dinner tables, sing old war songs, and recount their experiences. The annual state and national meetings, called encampments, attracted thousands of members, including Lucy, who attended many. Cities in twenty-two states from Maine to Oregon hosted the veterans. Railroads offered special discounted rates and scheduled special trains.

To promote charity, the organization set up funds for the relief of needy veterans, widows, and orphans. The funds could be used for medical, burial, and housing expenses and for purchases of food and household goods. Lucy may have been the recipient of this charity, as she eventually found work with the soldiers and received assistance toward her medical care and funeral expenses. Finally, to encourage loyalty, the GAR posts

Ribbons like this were worn by members of the GAR. Lucy wears a similar ribbon denoting herself a member of the Sanderson GAR in the only known photograph of her, dating to an 1898 GAR reunion. Collection of the Cultural Arts Center, Floyd County Library, New Albany, Indiana.

were committed to reminding citizens of the significance of a united nation. The organization commissioned monuments and memorials and encouraged the preservation of Civil War sites, relics, and documents.

In principle, the GAR was founded on the democratic concept that all honorably discharged Union veterans were eligible to join, and, as of 1871, all had equal standing in the GAR. In practice, though, individual posts developed their own systems of inclusion, exclusion, hierarchy, and equality. Contrary to assumption, the posts of the GAR in the border states, such as Indiana or Kentucky, were more sympathetic to African American soldiers and more likely to admit them into their ranks. Whether a GAR post admitted veterans of the USCT into integrated posts was a matter of political and social positioning—a barometer of their fears about poverty, ostracism, and, ultimately, segregation—despite the policy that "no distinction of race, color, or politics should debar any respectable veteran who honorably wore the Union Blue from joining the Grand Army." In many areas, there were all-Black posts that maintained their organization with relative autonomy. Each post and state branch, as well as the national encampment of the GAR, struggled with how or if they should admit Black soldiers while maintaining their white members.

It was the GAR that hosted a reenactment of the Grand Review parade in 1892. This time, twenty-seven years after the victory at Appomattox, the aging veterans of the USCT were finally recognized for their service and marched as one. While all GAR posts remembered the Civil War as a war to preserve the Union and grant emancipation, historians debate whether equality after emancipation was a central concern to the GAR. In Indiana, there were many integrated posts, though they were unsurprisingly farther from the shores of the contested spaces of the Ohio River near New Albany. There was an all-Black post of the GAR in nearby Jeffersonville, but it was the New Albany post of the GAR that embraced Lucy as one of their own.

Race was not the only factor that made Lucy's unofficial membership in the GAR notable. The Woman's Relief Corps (WRC)—the GAR women's auxiliary group that would eventually help secure pensions for nurses—also openly struggled with these issues, opting to have a "Detached Corps" that reported directly to the national organization.

Some branches, even in northern cities like Baltimore, declared there "can never be in our day a Department of white and colored Corps working together harmoniously" because of both social condition and pragmatic concerns, such as the inability for Black members to read and write. In contrast, WRC leader Annie Whittenmeyer declared that there was no distinction of race in her Pennsylvania branches and that the North should be able to follow suit.

The most outspoken proponent of race equality in the WRC was Julia Layton of Washington, D.C. She was born enslaved in Virginia, and her father purchased her freedom. She was the official organizer for Black women in the southern WRC, and her rebuke of the women was blistering. She said she came "not as a representative of a despised and ignorant race" as "depicted to you this morning" but as "a member of the Woman's Relief Corps, who joined it with the understanding that it was the one organization on the face of the globe that accorded a woman her right, be she black or white." It was not until 1906 that the WRC unequivocally accepted Black members in the organization without separation.

THE SANDERSON POST OF THE GAR

These qualities were emphasized in the local chapters, including the Sanderson Post of the GAR in New Albany, Indiana. The post of the GAR was named after Colonel William Lawrence Sanderson, commander of the Indiana 23rd Regiment, who distinguished himself after three years of service between 1861 and 1864. He was utterly devoted to his soldiers and his family. He returned home to New Albany after the war and was elected mayor. He died suddenly at the age of fifty-five.

Despite being the only female member of the post and unofficially recognized, the officers of the Indiana 23rd Regiment escorted Lucy to each meeting as though she were a queen, and she was given a post of honor on the speaker's stand. At annual state encampments and Decoration Day exercises, she always marched with the troops. One of the most enduring legacies of the GAR was the founding of Decoration Day on May 30, now known as Memorial Day. Inspired by women in southern states who decorated Confederate graves with flowers, General John A. Logan, commander in chief of the GAR, requested members of all posts to decorate the graves of their fallen comrades with flowers on May 30, 1868. Members of local posts throughout the nation visited veterans' graves, decorated them with flowers, and honored the dead with eulogies.

However, not all soldiers were equally honored by memorial festivities. In New Albany in 1869, the second year of celebrating Memorial Day, the newspaper received reports that a good number of citizens refused to participate in Decoration Day ceremonies because a large number of Black soldiers had been buried in the National Cemetery. As a solution, the Black women of the community were invited to decorate the graves of their fallen friends and relatives. The newspaper spares no ink in chastising the community members who refused to decorate the graves of Black soldiers, stating that they had to express "irrepressible contempt for that man or woman who can carry his or her class prejudices to the grave of one who fell in defense of the noblest cause for which armies ever battled," especially given that the burials of these "negro soldiers are in a department of the cemetery to themselves, so that the over-sensitive may not even be compelled to look upon the little green hillocks that mark the place where these dusky warriors sleep in death and dream of wars no more." If this anti-Black sentiment was so prevalent in Memorial Day services, there was certainly backlash to the status of Lucy in memorial services once she joined the festivities.

It seems, though, that Lucy was embraced as a full member. She attended nearly all the GAR reunions, but she must have been exceedingly proud to participate in the reunion of the soldiers of southern Indiana held in her hometown New Albany in August 1886. The entire town was "splendidly decorated" and cheerful with flags, banners, and evergreens decked out in red, white, and blue to celebrate the arrival of men for the four-day celebration, which included a speech from the governor. The events closed with appearances by the Knights of Pythias and a mock battle that entertained the crowds that gathered for closing ceremonies at the Camp Noble grounds. Despite the nefarious appearance of gambling tables, the reunion was deemed a success, and they resolved to hold it there again the following year.

Lucy also maintained a very close relationship with the soldiers throughout her life. Five or six years after the conclusion of the war,

Members of the Sanderson Post of the GAR in 1903, including many of the men who signed petitions on behalf of Lucy Nichols's pension request. Courtesy of the Floyd County Library, New Albany, Indiana.

she caught smallpox. It was a soldier who took her in, prepared a room for her, cared for her, and kept her from the pesthouse. She regularly attended reunions and actively participated in the community's acknowledgment of war veterans. According to a description in the newspaper of 1897, the bustling river town of New Albany patriotically transformed during Memorial Day festivities. Many homes and all the public buildings would wave "Old Glory." Citizens and GAR posts from the region would gather at the National Cemetery on Ekin Avenue. An orator, such as Reverend Dr. Ford of the Centenary United Methodist Church, would commemorate the day. The fire department, perhaps including Lucy's husband John, would present the veterans as the Crescent Band led the march. The GAR posts would march from their hall at the corner of Market and Pearl streets, surrounded by stirring music. The graves of soldiers were lovingly adorned with flowers and small flags. Described in 1897 were the "usual characters" of the Memorial Day ceremonies, and Lucy was undoubtedly present, deeply honored among her comrades.

In fact, another article in the *New Albany Evening Tribune* specifically recognizes Lucy's role in Memorial Day services in 1892. Lucy handed out boutonnieres to the veterans as they marched to Sunday memorial services at the Centenary Church the day before Memorial Day. It is very likely she also attended or even participated in the Memorial Day march to the National Soldiers' Cemetery in New Albany. Oral history states that she led the parades alongside the mayor. On Monday, May 30, a procession gathered at 1:00 in the afternoon at the corner of Pearl and Market streets in downtown New Albany to march to the cemetery on Ekin Avenue, some two miles away. It was a spectacular production. The GAR posts and the WRC were joined by the New Albany Division of the Uniform Rank of the Knights of Pythias. The Uniform Rank was a distinctive and higher rank of the Knights of Pythias, a national formalized drill corps known particularly for their distinctive costumes. The fire department led the march, "attired in their new spring uniforms and the apparatus was tastefully decorated," according to the *New Albany Evening Tribune*. Along the march route, they were joined by the GAR and Knights of Pythias from nearby Jeffersonville. Lucy was known for participating in all the parades, rumored to have worn her old "soldier clothes."

An "immense crowd" had gathered at the cemetery to greet the parade and participate in the memorial program. The ceremony's program was infused with both lively patriotism and somber remembrance. The Crescent Band welcomed the procession, a chorus sang "Cover Them Over" and "Columbia My Country," and Mrs. George T. Webster sang a solo of "Stars and Stripes Forever." From its inception in 1868, it was customary for Memorial Day celebrations to include impressive musical accompaniment and the best of speakers. Two chaplains led prayer and benediction, and soldiers past and present honored the fallen, scattering memorial flowers on the graves. It was a moving tribute to those who served.

Lucy was praised by her community, and her personal pride was noted again and again in the periodicals of the time. In 1894, she was at a reunion of soldiers seated with them under the parquet. During the festivities, Chaplain Woods, a veteran himself, acknowledged her hardships and service, and she rose to receive the cheers of the audience, which went on for several minutes. In 1897, members of the Sanderson Post presented Lucy with a "handsome rocking chair" as a "slight token of their appreciation." The event was marked by formalities where Lucy was escorted from the outpost by Senior V. C. Sharp, taken before the commander, and eventually presented the chair by Comrade Ford. In a rare quote from Lucy, she replied, overwhelmed and surprised, "I thank you, and I appreciate the gift."

Lucy's positive presence extended far beyond the local New Albany community. An 1889 article in the *New Albany Evening Tribune* explains that she was personally acquainted with General Benjamin Harrison and planned to attend his inauguration as the twenty-third president of the United States on March 4, 1889, although it does not seem she actually attended the inauguration.

As the GAR matured in the 1870s, it took on a political dimension beyond its fraternal aims. Local, state, and national GAR realized the power of collective action, especially as it related to pension legislation. Meanwhile, Lucy continued to build strong relationships with the

Downtown New Albany, Lucy's hometown after the Civil War, as captured by C. Heimberger and Son, Pearl Street north from Main Street, New Albany, Indiana, ca. 1890. Courtesy of the Floyd County Library, New Albany, Indiana.

veterans and met generals and future presidents. With these powerful connections at her disposal, Lucy mounted a multiyear battle with the Federal Bureau of Pensions that goes all the way to the president's desk.

5

A PENSION FOR ARMY NURSES

HOPING TO RECRUIT SOLDIERS AND PROLONG THEIR SERVICE DURING the Revolutionary War in 1776, the Continental Congress promised disability and retirement pensions. Benefits expanded to soldiers' widows and orphans in the War of 1812. In 1861, Congress enacted the first Civil War pension act, granting existing benefits to new enlistees and extending benefits to widows and heirs if a soldier died in uniform as a measure to ensure soldiers their immediate female family members would be cared for in the case of their death. The list of eligible pensioners expanded in stages through 1890 to even include male kin. By that point, the pension system consumed more than 40 percent of the government budget, funding more than 960,000 pensions, with thousands more awaiting processing. While the pension system emerges as an important cross-racial and cross-class step in America's welfare system, it was not without deeply rooted prejudices. However, there was one group of dedicated women whose sacrifices went unacknowledged by the Pension Bureau for nearly three decades: more than 18,000 Union hospital workers, including Black nurses, laundresses, and cooks.

Female nurses of the Civil War, mainly white and middle class, began arguing for nurses' pensions as early as the 1870s. More than financial remuneration, women wanted validation that a nurse's work fighting disease and healing the wounded was as important to winning the war as a soldier's service on the battlefield. The government resisted, insisting that military and what they deemed as civilian work remain separate. It was not until 1901 that Congress passed an act that would guarantee that all women in the U.S. Army Nurse Corps would have military status. But in 1890, no bill yet existed that would categorically provide women, including female nurses that had served in any American war, with a pension independent of her relation to a man.

It was the collective power of women's advocacy groups that would finally sway the hearts and minds of government officials that nurses deserved a pension, but it was a decades-long battle. The process can be traced back to the war itself, when women's charitable groups formed across the nation to address the shortage of army supplies, sanitation, and medical treatment needs of the soldiers, giving women the skill sets to both administer charities and navigate male-dominated wartime systems. After the war, many women's groups formed or reassessed their mission to provide critical services to army veterans and their families. By 1869, women's groups were addressing many critical needs of veterans, orphans, and former nurses, including poverty and homelessness. Their devotion was rooted in both personal connections to soldiers and a sense of patriotic duty.

While an ailing Lucy labored away in post–Civil War New Albany, Indiana, women across the nation lobbied for her right to receive a pension—though early versions of the legislation considered only those nurses, typically white and middle class, who were formally registered by the army. Two influential women's groups—the Pension and Relief Committee of the Woman's Relief Corps (WRC) and the Army Nurses' Association of Washington—along with passionate individuals such as Civil War nurse Mary Ann Bickerdyke—spearheaded efforts to secure nurses' pensions. The task ahead was monumental, taking decades of debates, petitions, false starts, and compromises to see it to fruition.

The first local WRC group formed in Maine in 1869 with the goal of maintaining a social community supporting soldiers and their families. The WRC became a widespread phenomenon, with local and state chapters cropping up nationwide. Some were under the aegis of local Grand Army of the Republic (GAR) posts, while others were independent. WRC leadership quickly realized that if they wanted to successfully impact the lives of veterans and remain viable, they needed the support and approval of the largest veterans' organization. The women met with some resistance: from the perspective of conservative male veterans in the GAR, women would disrupt their fraternal bond and network of support. Some men also feared that women participating in such a charitable endeavor would lead to other, riskier activism, such as suffrage.

In 1882, the National Encampment of the GAR struck down a resolution to form the Woman's National Relief Corps as an auxiliary of the GAR. According to Commander in Chief George S. Merrill, men needed a group formed only by those who shared the unique bond of military service. Most women did not see combat and therefore, by Merrill's logic, could not belong to a group that was composed of only veteran soldiers. In the fall of 1882, Kate B. Sherwood was appointed editor of the women's section of the nationally distributed *National Tribune* out of Washington, D.C., and a powerful press campaign began.

Despite the skepticism and hurdles, the women of state and local WRC chapters prevailed in their efforts, insisting they were as willing to serve the Union soldiers postwar as they were during the war. Beyond their devoted charitable work, the women of the WRC shared the desire to preserve the memory of the war and promote patriotism. In 1883, fifty delegates from WRC state departments and other Union relief organizations met in Denver for the GAR National Encampment. Much work had been done to drum up support for the establishment of the national WRC organization, but there were lingering doubts. The GAR vote was divided over who qualified for membership to the national auxiliary. Eventually, they recognized that limiting membership in the WRC to families of veterans would constrain fundraising and the potential impact of the group because it was, after all, the poor families of veterans that they wished to serve. If they limited membership to families, there would be a practical financial limitation.

Ultimately, the convention passed the resolution unanimously to form the national organization, which was open to all women who

Kate B. Sherwood, writer for and founder of the Women's Relief Corps, from *Local and National Poets of America*, edited by Thomas William Herringshaw. New York: American Publisher's Association, 1890.

supported Union soldiers and their families (though the competitive Ladies' GAR formed with more restrictive membership). Although the WRC was formed primarily under the auspices of veteran support, they also took up the cause to "cherish and emulate the deeds of the army nurses, and all loyal women who rendered loving service during the war." Their membership, which reached about 100,000 in the 1890s, was formed by loyal northern women, including many widows, mothers, and sisters of Union veterans, as well as former army nurses.

Meanwhile, in 1881, Dorothea Dix, former superintendent of women nurses in the army, and Harriett Patience Dame, a Civil War nurse, worked together to launch a social and advocacy group supporting nurses that began as the Ex-Army Nurses' Association and eventually coalesced into the Association of Army Nurses (later the National Association of Army Nurses [NAAN]). The WRC and the NAAN, though sometimes at odds about the details, rallied together to fight for a nurses' pension.

Debates in the House about the merits of awarding pensions to army nurses began as early as 1882, when the Senate referred Senate Bill 1305 providing payment of female nurses during the war to the Committee on Military Affairs. According to the *Congressional Record* of March 17, 1882, Mr. Logan of the Committee on Military Affairs reported "adversely," and the bill was "postponed indefinitely." While the records pertaining to the deliberation of the Committee on Military Affairs no longer exist, it's pretty clear that the Pension and Relief Committee of the WRC was actively engaged in the debate because they sent a prompt rebuttal letter to the Office of the Secretary on March 29, 1882, less than two weeks after the Senate meeting report. The Relief Committee includes at least one recognizable name, Clara Barton, who would fight for relief for a decade and go on to establish the Red Cross. Despite these early efforts, it would take a few years before the petitions and activism on behalf of a pension would gain real traction.

In 1884, WRC National Senior Vice President Kate B. Sherwood put forward a plan to create a general relief fund that would provide a yearly sum to former nurses at Christmas as a stopgap measure. Hundreds of letters flooded the WRC from hopeful former nurses who believed relief was imminent. Unfortunately, the WRC was not in a financial position to provide the relief that the nurses expected, and little was done for the next two years. The WRC renewed commitment to lobbying for the Army Nurses Pension Act in 1886, but they needed a way to address the overwhelming and immediate need. They promoted the filing of pension requested through special acts of Congress, which were processed by the House and Senate independent of Pension Bureau standards. The House had been considering individual requests for nurses' pensions for decades, approving some on special merit and others perhaps on favoritism (who-knows-who scenarios).

The WRC invested time and resources to encourage and facilitate these applications from army nurses but only if they fit a very specific model. By repeatedly promoting the ideal angelic Victorian nurse to Congress—a benevolent, selfless, white middle-class woman who fell on hard times postwar—the WRC appealed to male chivalry and built the argument for the morally deserving nurse. Few of the nurses' pension requests that made it to the floor were rejected. Many of those pensions were approved at $20 or $25 per month, or double the amount ultimately proposed in the compromised bill. But the House and Congress grew tired of considering special requests for nurses' pensions on an individual basis. One of the motivating factors for considering a nurses' pension bill was whether Congress wanted to continue, much to their inconvenience, to consider each pension request individually (at their Friday afternoon session no less). These special acts of Congress would come to plague the House and Senate as the only means for army nurses to receive pensions, taking up valuable legislative time.

The WRC tactic was smart: the individual private pension requests for nurses that were awarded by special acts of Congress set a precedent that paved the way for the Army Nurses Pension Act to pass. Support for army nurses' pensions was widespread among Republicans and with the GAR but with limitations. In 1886, the GAR's primary objective was to push through legislation that benefited a larger demographic of dependents of veterans, and they could not fully support the act at the sacrifice of their broader initiative.

The women who composed the WRC Pension Committee were revolutionary and resilient: in an era with limited rights for women and no ability to vote or hold office, they forged a path to the nurses' pension by negotiating with the Senate Pension Committee and the House Committee on Invalid Pensions. Appealing to their morality and sentiment, the first sincere attempt at passing an Army Nurses Pension Act in 1888 was tabled by the Senate Pension Committee because the WRC failed to definitively outline how many women stood to benefit from the act and what the cost would be to the government.

With this defeat and stagnant progress in the coming year, Kate B. Sherwood stepped down as the head of the WRC, replaced by Annie Wittenmyer, who galvanized the committee and made fast progress. In 1888, the WRC, which had grown to about 100,000 members, circulated a petition supporting a pension of $25 per month for nurses, gathering 160,000 signatures in two weeks. They also lobbied their representatives, garnering widespread support. If the women of the WRC could not be in the room when the bill was considered, they would, in the words of Wittenmyer, produce a "petition so long it will girdle the Capital and show our legislators that the country demands some measure of relief in behalf of the distresses and neglected woman patriots of the war." In 1890, Senate Bill 945, granting a nurses' pension, passed through the Senate and would be considered by the House. But with the staggering estimates of nearly 900 nurses of as many as 22,000 eligible, according to the War Department, the bill was summarily ignored.

Recognizing this defeat, the WRC compromised with the NAAN and the GAR to put forward yet another series of bills that reduced the amount from $25 per month to $12 per month, and they mobilized a team of women to reside in Washington to lobby. The Butler Bill, as it came to be known, was put forward first to the House of Representatives, then to the Senate. While the WRC and NAAN were indispensable to the process, they ultimately were not allowed in the room where the fate of hundreds of nurses would be decided. Some in the House recognized this contradiction, including Representative George Washington Smith, a Republican from Illinois. He said, "I regard it as a grander thing to stand up for a woman who is not entitled to the right to vote and who cannot be heard in person on this floor."

The House of Representatives met on June 28, 1892, during the first session of the 52nd Congress. After the entirety of the House finished business for the day, the House broke out into a meeting of the Committee of the Whole, a powerful body that considered legislation that would be proposed to House members. Civil War pension matters were under the jurisdiction of the Committee on Invalid Pensions, a standing committee of the House of Representatives formed in 1831 to report general and special bills authorizing the payments of pensions. Originally, the committee was formed to oversee all pension requests, but duties were narrowed in 1867 to address the flood of Civil War pension requests.

Augustus N. Martin, a Civil War veteran, Democrat from Indiana, and chair of the Committee on Invalid Pensions, brought House Resolution 7294 before the Committee of the Whole. The bill read,

> Be it enacted, etc., That every Woman who served as an army nurse in the actual personal care and nursing of the sick and wounded during the civil war, either in field or general hospitals of the United States, and who continued in such care and nursing of the Sick and wounded not less than six months, and who are without other adequate means of support than their own daily labor, shall, upon making due proof of the fact, according to such rules and regulations as the Secretary of the Interior may provide, be placed upon the pension roll of the United States and be entitled to receive $12 per month; and such pension shall commence from the date of filing the application, in the Pension Office after the passage of this act: Provided, That any pension granted under any former law to any applicant under this act shall terminate from the date of commencement of the pension under this act: Provided further, That no person now receiving a pension as army nurse under any special act shall be entitled to receive a pension under this act.

Martin, as chair of the committee, then read a report written by Iowa Democrat Walter Halben Butler. The report states that, through the best authorities of the WRC and the Association of Army Nurses, no more than 300 women would qualify, and, to their best estimate, only 150 women would. He makes a moving tribute in his report, appealing to both the pragmatic concerns of cost and the sentiments, chivalry, and morals of the men in the House:

> This small band of noble women are the sole remaining representatives of a class of patriotic women who came from every Section of Our land. In their service they knew no North, no South. As angels of mercy they came to care for and comfort both blue and gray. They ministered to the needs of the suffering everywhere. On field or in hospital their sweet

voices were heard, and their gentle touch was given to assuage Sorrow and pain.

Few members of the Committee of the Whole denied that the services rendered by women nurses were valuable, even indispensable, to Union victory, but there was much debate about whether they should be compensated. Could women nurses be paid pensions for army service when they were, in actuality, ineligible to enlist? And should the House decide they could, where would the line be drawn between those eligible and those ineligible for pensions? Democrats, adamantly opposed to unnecessary pensioning, controlled the House. The bill was swimming in unfavorable waters.

The meeting got quite boisterous; multiple calls for order were issued, shouts of "veto!" rang through the House, and rounds of applause followed passionate pleas on behalf of the nurses. Genial, half-good-hearted jokes prompted bouts of laughter. Despite the gentlemanly formalities and raucous outbursts, the business at hand was serious. Not only were these former nurses unable to care for themselves and a burden to society and women's charity groups, but the decision of the House was a reflection on the government's system of valuing women and their work.

The Committee of the Whole had many questions and quarrels. Among them, had nurses been previously compensated? Perhaps women could simply be reimbursed for out-of-pocket expenses. In an exchange between Butler and Leonidus F. Livingston, a Georgia Democrat, on this subject, Livingston asked, "Were they not paid for [their service]?" Butler replied, "No, most of them were not paid, but instead of being paid spent their own money for food and medicine for the sick and wounded soldiers." In a particularly snarky response, Mr. Livingston declared, "Well, let them bring in an account against the Government and I will vote to pay the money back." Another amendment proposed to the bill required that no person who had been paid for their service during the war would be allowed pension, which was also struck down. It was argued that their pay was so "meager" that no nurse entered into the position for the pay. Indeed, some nurses, if they had been properly registered through the surgeon general's office or one of the charitable groups, might have been paid an inconsistent and paltry sum, but representatives urged their peers to remember that soldiers received a pension despite having been paid during their time of service.

Would passing this pension bill snowball into pension requests from other nonmilitary personnel who served the cause? If the government provided pensions for nurses, would telegraphers, washerwomen, or cooks also qualify? Butler denies this possibility, distinguishing the service of nurses: "The women who attended the sick and wounded soldiers were as much doing duty for their country, and doing real warfare, you may say, as soldiers on the front."

How would the government pay for the additional pensions? At this very meeting of the House, they appropriated $134,000,000, more than 40 percent of the federal budget, to cover swelling pension requests, and now they would add even more to that staggering amount. Pensions were paid, after all, by working Americans who contributed to the tax coffers. Democrat Elisha D. Meredith of Virginia was the most vocally opposed to the bill for many reasons, including the financial burden to the taxpayers, which was "impossible to meet" over the next decade with soldier pensions alone. As a southern Democrat, he also pointed out that no nurse from his state requested a pension despite often caring for Union troops. Meredith struggled to rectify that people of the South were required to pay into a government pension system that did not benefit his constituents.

Meredith's monologue so annoyed his fellow committee members that a vote on the issue was raised just to shut his remarks down. Ultimately, the Committee of the Whole passed a favorable recommendation of the bill, with 125 yeas, 56 nays, and 147 not voting. The bill headed for approval by the Senate, which had passed the same bill two years prior. It should have been a breeze.

The Senate Committee on Pensions presented an amended version of House Resolution 7294. The critical change was to limit eligibility for the pension to those officially employed by the surgeon general. Limiting those who would qualify had an enormous impact: few regimental nurses, laundresses, and cooks, especially those who had escaped from slavery like Lucy, were officially employed. It's hard to determine just how many women were affected by this decision, but Senator James Berry Henderson, a Democrat from Arkansas who was opposed to the bill, reported some staggering numbers. According to War Department records, there were 497 hired white nurses and 281 Black nurses. Add to those rosters those hired by Dorothea Dix under the surgeon general (371 white nurses), the Sisters of Charity (248 white nurses), and the Sanitary Commission (another 31 white nurses) and, by order of the surgeon general, another 95 white nurses. All of these had some official records supporting service, but almost all were white. Berry added to that an estimated 4,556 white and 138 Black "undetermined" nurses who were hired under unknown authority. The numbers don't exactly add up and probably scarcely address the women in the field, but Berry totals the potential list of pensioners at more than 6,000. These overwhelming numbers scared his fellow senators, who were more apt to support a very restrictive definition of service under the surgeon general than to allow the possible deluge of requests allowed under the House of Representatives version.

The more restrictive version of the bill was presented to the Senate on July 26, 1892. The debate got off to a rocky start. Senator Berry vehemently opposed the bill because the women "were not soldiers, but were simply nurses during the late war." With an indifference to the unique horrors of wartime service, he asked why Civil War nurses should be compensated differently from the women who daily care for the sick in hospitals across the nation. Delaware Democratic Senator George Gray supported Senator Berry's position. Forgoing "chivalry" and "gallantry," he opposed the bill, questioning whether the average American should be asked to pay for this addition to the pension rolls, which would be, in his opinion, a slippery slope.

To these objections, Republican leader of the Senate Committee on Pensions Cushman Davis of Minnesota replied,

> There is a vast difference, inappreciative to the Senator from Delaware, between the services which nurses in civil life perform in city hospitals and the services of those women who followed our Army into the field, who were the very angels of battle and desolation. . . . They

were implored by those in the front to come and render their service of benefaction and care. They did not do it in the bosom of peace; it was done sometimes under fire, in hospital tents, under every disadvantage . . . and not only to the soldier of one side, but to the soldier of both indiscriminately.

Davis's impassioned speech must have swayed the minds and hearts of the majority of the Senate. Despite very vocal objections from a few Democratic senators, the Senate agreed to the amended version of the bill and sent it to conference with the House. The House and Senate came to agreement on the amendments.

Nearly thirty years after the Civil War, in an overdue acknowledgment of women's work, the Army Nurses Pension Act was finally passed on August 5, 1892. The provision made monthly pensions of $12 available to nurses who had served for at least six months and could no longer "earn a support." The act stipulated that nurses "who rendered service as nurses in attendance upon the sick or wounded in any regimental, post or camp, or general hospital of the armies" had to be "employed by the Surgeon General of the Army as nurses, under contract or otherwise."

This was a decisive victory for the WRC, NAAN, GAR, and the hundreds of women who would benefit from the diligent advocacy. Yet the compromises made to get the bill passed, such as restrictive qualifications and a lower pension payout, left many women vulnerable. Years earlier, in a foreboding 1890 letter to the Senate, Annie Wittenmyer expressed concern about these same restrictions. She recognized early on that efforts to limit the bill to officially contracted nurses would substantially restrict the list of eligible women. Her words have an ominous effect when she wrote, "I can not but feel a deep anxiety in this bill." Wittenmyer's anxiety was warranted. Women such as Lucy, who did not fit within the limited definitions of the bill, stood against an enormous bureaucratic machine intent to narrow the field of eligible pensioners.

6

CLAIM 1130541

THE FIGHT FOR A PENSION

IN SEPTEMBER 1892, ONE MONTH AFTER THE ARMY NURSES PENSION Act was passed, Lucy submitted her first request for a pension. She was not alone—an estimated one in seven female hospital attendants eventually applied for a pension after Congress passed the legislation. Because Lucy could not read, one of the men with whom she served or a member of the Sanderson Grand Army of the Republic (GAR) post must have shared the good news with her—and quickly. Lucy had to mobilize a team of people, gather the financial resources, and take the time away from daily work to submit her request. Lucy had to employ the services of a third-party notary, a white man, to transcribe her depositions, and she had to find transportation to the notary's office. In addition, she had to secure witnesses who could attest to her identity. Add to this the complication that the law stipulated that no lawyer, casually known as pension sharks, could receive more than $10 in a pension case so as to avoid taking advantage of pensioners and, by extension, the American tax dollar. The result, however, was that pension lawyers had to take on cases essentially for free. Additionally, the Pension Office recognized early on that the records of former slaves' service were very meager, and they established restrictive policies to avoid fraudulent claims made by dishonest claim agents. The road ahead for Lucy's claim was fraught with obstacles.

In general, pension applications were costly endeavors, and cost could pose a significant barrier for many poor Black applicants, who were awarded pensions disproportionately compared to their white counterparts. With an average yearly income for Black families of about $250 per year, Lucy might not have been able to afford the costs associated with pension applications if it weren't for her close connections with GAR veterans. Even with their help, she probably had to incur expenses without being fully confident she would be rewarded for her effort. Pension lawyers usually worked on contingency, meaning they got some or all of their payment from the first pension check. In addition to the fees associated with the lawyer, pension applicants sometimes had travel expenses, which included visiting witnesses for their claims and doctor visits for evaluation and testimony. They often had to secure the services of a notary, and the notary charged more for illiterate customers.

Lucy was more fortunate than others in this challenging situation because she was in friendly company and in close contact with her veteran peers. She arrived in the office of notary and pension attorney Benjamin F. Welker in downtown New Albany with her two witnesses: Lafayette Frederick and Louis C. Hipple. Both Welker and Frederick, who was a major real estate agent in New Albany, had served with Lucy in the Civil War and had known her for about thirty years. Hipple was a dray driver, or drayman, who drove goods via wagons pulled by horses, probably to the river port or rail yards for shipment. He had known Lucy for more than twenty years. Both were white males accompanying a Black woman to see a white notary. A pro forma Declaration for Nurses Pension was filed on September 5, 1892, by Welker on behalf of Lucy Nichols, who signed her name with an "X" because she could neither read nor write. The underlined portions of her declaration were completed by the notary, and the remaining segments were preprinted. Her declaration read, "Lucy Nichols (formerly Lucy Higgs) aged about 52 years, a resident of New Albany, county of Floyd State of Indiana, who, being duly sworn according to law, declares that she is the identical Lucy Higgs who was employed as Nurse by appointment on or about the first day of July

Civil War Veteran and GAR member Lafayette Frederick in 1903. He helped Lucy
submit pension applications and served as a witness. Detail from Sanderson GAR
Post Memorial Picture. Courtesy of the Floyd County Library, New Albany, Indiana.

1862." Nothing in this document actually identifies Lucy as a woman
who escaped slavery to join the regiment as a nurse, but there are subtle
clues in her application.

Lucy did not know her own age, nor did she know the exact date
on which she joined the regiment. Enslaved people were often unaware
of their birth date. Most former slaves who filed pension requests could
offer only an approximation of their age. Slave cultures were based largely
on oral histories, and they marked time differently than those who could
read or write. Typically, in oral cultures, events were marked by their
approximations in time to other events. Her birth year is known only

posthumously through the property inventories of her owners. Lucy was also "appointed" to the position of nurse because she could not, as a Black woman, officially be contracted to serve as nurse. Although Lucy probably felt security and honor in this unofficial appointment, it was never legally documented. Not only did Lucy have to prove her service without required documentation, but she had to justify her worth as a Black woman as well.

Her declaration continues, "She was honorably released at Indianapolis, Ind, on or about the 23rd day of July 1865. That she is physically unable to earn a support by reason of Disease of throat, Rheumatism, and general debility. That said disabilities are to the best of her knowledge and belief of a permanent character." With an "X," Lucy swore that her service period and ailments qualified her for a pension under the Army Nurses Pension Act as passed in 1892, and her two witnesses, friends of decades, attested to the veracity of Lucy's identity.

A woman's sworn word, however, proved insufficient evidence for a pension claim. The Pension Office was reluctant to use oral history or firsthand accounts as evidence in claims, in part because there was no opportunity for cross-examination. Only written record evidence was free from any suspicion. Like many other women who served as a nurse in the Civil War, especially Black nurses and those traveling with regiments, Lucy did not have documentation to support her claim. The response to Lucy's first request for an "Invalid Pension" filed on August 5, 1892, seems to approve her claim, awarding her $12 per month. Under the "Approvals" section, Lucy's pension was "Approved for admission" but then was struck through: "Admission Rejection. Claimant not employed as a nurse by proper authority." What were the conditions under which her application was first approved and then summarily rejected? It is possible that Lucy's illiteracy signaled to the reviewers that Lucy was of a lower social status and therefore less likely to have been appointed to the position of nurse and a less credible claimant. In addition, the standardized forms left little room for Lucy to provide any narrative particular to her case. It is unclear whether the reviewers were aware of the race of their applicants, but it is certain that Lucy's words were always filtered through the white notary who documented her claims.

The War Department's Records and Pension Division ultimately denied her request for the first time on October 22, 1892, writing "no record found" on a form that was made to process the claims of male veterans. Despite dedicating three years of her life to nursing sick and wounded soldiers and losing her young daughter Mona on the battle trail, no physical records and no official scrap of written evidence survived.

The faulty process to secure a nurses' pension favored upper-class white women. During the Civil War, incoming nurses were processed and categorized by Dorothea Dix, superintendent of women nurses for the Union under the surgeon general. Mostly white women of elevated social status were appointed as official hospital nurses, and they were properly documented as such. Women of color or lower social status were usually assigned hospital positions as laundresses or cooks even though they often functioned in a similar capacity to nurses. Their service, however, was not systematically documented. Outside of the official hospitals, regimental nurses traveled with the troops, most serving as laundresses and cooks in addition to caring for the sick and wounded. Their records are even more sporadic, and their service was perceived as less valuable.

The classifications and systems for processing incoming nurses had many consequences. If records existed at all for regimental nurses and hospital laundresses and cooks, they often presented inaccurate descriptions of the scope of the women's work. These labels devalued their service and ultimately jeopardized any future pension requests. The lower the status of position, the less likely that there was any official documentation of service. As "contraband of war," the lowest of stations, Lucy's appointment to the position of nurse was never documented for posterity or for verification of service. For those Black women who joined the regimental ranks, they had added burdens to their claims: few could read or write, making them reliant on notaries to transcribe their claims. They also usually needed to secure the services of a pension lawyer. They rarely had the option of advocating on their own behalf.

After the passage of the 1892 act, many former hospital laundresses and cooks made claims that their work differed little from nurses. To secure a pension, they had to provide witness from "competent authority"—usually white men, preferably doctors, who were directly associated with the hospitals where women served. Essentially, each claim presented for a pension was a test of the claimant's honesty. The prevalent logic used in the evaluation of claims was that intelligence or the perception of such through the ability to read and write was an indication of honesty. In a society that believed that character was linked to intelligence and that intelligence was linked to race, being an illiterate Black woman was a significant disadvantage. For regimental nurses such as Lucy, the struggle was even greater. Their names were not listed on official hospital registers, and regimental nurses were uniformly classified as laundresses, leading to misconceptions about the value of their work. Additionally, it was unlikely that a regimental nurse would have maintained contact with the doctor under whom she served, but she needed his "competent authority" to testify to her service.

By 1893, the Army Nurses Pension Act already required revision. It was expanded to provide pensions to nurses who had not been officially appointed by the surgeon general, and they broadened the range of eligible witnesses who could verify service. "Competent authority" witnesses now included the testimony of soldiers with whom the nurses had served or female coworkers, both groups that nurses more likely had contact with postwar. While the bureau broadened the pool of eligible applicants and witnesses, they still held authority to determine the credibility of the witnesses. Because Lucy had chosen to live in New Albany near many of the veterans of the Indiana 23rd Regiment, she not only maintained contact with them but also worked in their homes as domestic help.

In the wake of Lucy's first denial, the first wave of affidavits from members of the Indiana 23rd filed in support of Lucy's request came from Lorenzo D. Emory and Spencer Byrn, M.D., in 1893. Dr. Byrn, a surgeon with the troop from September 26, 1862, through August 9, 1863, certified Lucy as a nurse with the regiment, stating that she "was a good true and faithful nurse rendering great aid and comfort to sick and disabled soldiers." From Dr. Byrn's testimony, Lucy was clearly a valued and trusted member of the team that supported ailing soldiers. The notary concludes the statement with the phrase, "He states the above facts to be true as he destinctly [sic] remembers."

It was insufficient for a surgeon to simply submit a sworn written testimonial. The bureau investigated the character of the testimonials, rating Dr. Byrn as "good" but also to call into question the validity of the statements in subtle and suggestive ways. A follow-up letter to Dr. Byrn questions if the testimonial was based on records or on memory regardless of the clear statement that it was based on memory. Implicit in that is the suggestion that his memory is an unsatisfactory stand-in for a written record.

The general affidavit of Lorenzo D. Emory of January 23, 1893, is questioned similarly. Emory, arguably one of Lucy's biggest champions in the process, served in the Civil War between 1861 and 1864 and was honorably discharged. He himself received a pension of $40 per month that he secured in the 1880s, so he had some perspective on the process that Lucy was undertaking. Emory testified under oath that while he was an orderly in the Indiana 23rd Regiment in Bolivar, Tennessee, "M Brucker," the regiment's surgeon, "assigned" Lucy "to duty in the Regimental Hospital as nurse," where she remained until the regiment mustered out. After Lorenzo Emory's service was confirmed by the Department of the Interior, the commissioner of the department's Bureau of Pensions also sent Emory a follow-up letter that further prods Lorenzo's testimony, asking him to advise as to the "exact nature of the duties performed." The letter inquires, suggestively, "Did she personally wait and attend upon the sick and wounded, or were her duties practically those of a cook and laundress?" The bureau assumes, despite testimonials of two soldiers of "competent authority," that women who served in regimental hospitals were not nurses but *merely* laundresses and cooks. Again, this reinforced the idea that official (white) nurses were worthy of compensation but that laundresses and cooks (typically Black) were not.

Perhaps Emory was perturbed by this further inquisition to his testimony because he sent a curt response in his own hand that simply stated, "The withen claiment Did Wait on the Sick and Wounded personally to my own personal knowledge and observation," signed "Lorenzo D. Emory." This short personal note was accompanied by a lengthier notarized general affidavit dated September 13, 1893.

Meanwhile, the Pension Office pursued other questions. In a letter of June 17, 1893, to the second auditor of the Treasury Department, the Bureau of Pensions inquires when Lucy was paid by the Treasury for her service as a nurse or otherwise. Something about this inquiry seems insincere because it seems pretty clear by this point that Lucy would never have been paid because she was not officially enrolled as an army nurse in a hospital. Furthermore, whether she had been paid was not a qualifying factor per the long arguments in the House Committee of the Whole. The Treasury Department replied, "No record of any fragment has been found on file in this office to Lucy Higgs." It goes on to suggest, ironically and inaccurately, that the Bureau of Pensions ask the surgeon general's office for proof of service. Had they received the memo that the scope of competent authority had been expanded by the surgeon general's office? Of course, the reply from the surgeon general's office, stamped July 6, 1893, says simply, "No records found in this case."

Shortly thereafter, on July 29, 1893, Lucy submitted a second general affidavit in reply to a letter, now lost, sent to her by the Bureau of Pensions. The affidavit states that Lucy "was employed by Magnus Brucker who was the Surgeon General of the 23rd Regt Indiana vol Inf. who stated to affiant that she would be regularly paid but that she never was paid anything by the government for her services as such nurse. That she had no written appointment as such nurse. The duties she performed in the hospital was giving medicine to sick soldiers, washed them and cooked for them and various other like duties that was necessary to be performed." Once again, she signed with an "X."

In November 1893, a memo to the Commissioner of Pensions confirms that the surgeon general's office reports "By Army Regulations 1863. par. 1293, it was provided that the senior medical officer will select the cooks, nurses, and matrons" and later confirms that Magnus Brucker, deceased by 1893, was indeed the surgeon who would have such a responsibility for the Indiana 23rd Regiment. Four days later, Lucy submitted her third affidavit. And in January 1894, Lucy's medical doctor of sixteen years, William A. Burney, also submitted a physician's affidavit verifying chronic diarrhea and rheumatism that prevented her from performing the manual labor that provided her livelihood.

and *she* further says that *her* knowledge of the above facts is obtained from the following sources, viz: *that she is the Claimant and states from her best recollection*

and that he has no interest nor concern in this matter.

James H. James
Attest—When Affiant signs by mark, two persons sign.

Lawrence B. Huckeby
Attest—When Affiant signs by mark, two persons sign.

Lucy X Nichols formerly Higgs
mark
Signature of Affiant.

Sworn to and subscribed before me this day by the above named Affiant; and I read affidavit to said Affiant and acquainted h*er* with its contents before *S* he executed the same. I further certify that I am in no wise interested in this case, nor am I concerned in its prosecution, and that said Affiant is personally known to me, that *S* he is a creditable person and so reputed in the community in which *S* he resides.

Witness my hand and official seal, this *8th* day of *Nov* , 18*93*.

B. F. Walker
Signature of Official.
Notary Public

L. S.

Signed with an "X" in 1893 because she could not read or write, Lucy's name appears on the affidavit with "formerly Higgs," connecting her to her history of enslavement under the Higgs family.

For more than a year already, Lucy and her numerous "competent authorities" testified to and reaffirmed her service, her "debility," her reputation, and her worthiness for a pension. Still insufficient, in January

1894, Lucy submitted another official declaration. This time, Lucy had to prove that her husband, John Nichols, who served in the U.S. Colored Infantry, had never received a pension and that she had no male heirs. Why John did not pursue a pension or apparently did not join the nearest Black GAR post in Jeffersonville, Indiana, is unclear. It is possible that they did not have the financial resources necessary to pursue his application. Regardless, Lucy's claim was considered secondary to male service. In all of this communication between government authorities, Lucy, and the soldiers, it is remarkable that the issue of color never obviously emerged. Nowhere in the surviving communication is there mention of Lucy's enslavement. Nowhere is there mention of Lucy's skin color—until this affidavit in January 1894, where she notes her husband's service in the USCT. It's possible that Lucy received coaching from one of the notaries or the Pension Office to carefully craft her statements to avoid the subject.

The same "Invalid Pension" form that was stamped "REJECTED" also contains a handwritten note that the request was "resubmitted for special examination Mar 8/94." Another similar form was boldly stamped "~~REJECTED~~ RE-OPENED." Lucy received official notice that the Commissioner of Pensions would conduct a special examination of her claim beginning on April 12, 1894, in New Albany, and she was invited to be present "in person or by attorney" to provide material evidence and cross-examine witnesses. She acknowledged receipt of the notification with an "X," requesting examination to begin "at once." Undoubtedly, that signature was imbued with great hope for her financial security and affirmation.

With news of the pending special examination received, there is a flurry of depositions made in support of her claims. On the same day that the special examination notification was stamped, two soldiers filed their depositions, and the following day, three more did so. In total, seven soldiers filed depositions in the month of April 1894. Lucy must have been rallying the support of her troops, waiting for the opportunity to make a strong case. Lucy maintained long-term and regular contact with the soldiers to find them so readily available.

Charles E. Villier submitted a lengthy deposition on Lucy's behalf. A fifty-one-year-old farmer living in New Albany in 1894, he reflected back on Lucy's service to the troops in some detail. She was first a laundress for the soldiers, eventually earning her position in the regimental hospital. Villier himself had witnessed nurse Lucy at work when she dispensed his dose of medicine, and she cared for him when he came down with fever. She was, according to his memory, consistently with the troops once she joined them in Bolivar. His testimony affirms her work, consistency, and dedication. John Sandlewick, a sixty-year-old flagman for the Dinky Train, wrote in his deposition of April 13, 1894, that Lucy was "a useful and industrious nurse."

Benjamin F. Welker, the same attorney and notary public who helped Lucy submit her first claim, provided new details to Lucy's service in his deposition dated April 13, 1894. As a mail carrier for the regiment, he regularly witnessed Lucy in the hospital and asked where to find the sick soldiers, and he was given medicine by Lucy. He adds a personal laudatory message that distinguishes his testimony, writing, "She was a success—an excellent nurse; I often heard the Doctor say he could not get along without the assistance of claimant. She always knew what to do, and was attentive and ready." Physician John S. McPheeters, who had charge of the regiment's hospital along with Dr. Brucker, attested that Lucy was "always ready to obey any order given her as far as the sick was concerned. . . . She was as thoroughly under the contract of the hospital authorities as if she had been authoritatively employed." Lucy's doctor also submits another testimony, confirming her debilities and that she is unable to do the manual labor needed for sustenance despite being "quite poor."

The depositions made that April were transcribed and certified by George M. Moore, signed "Geo M Moore," special examiner with the Board of Reviews. Moore personally met Lucy, the only clear evidence of an official in the case meeting with Lucy directly. Local claims agents typically represented law firms based in Washington, D.C., and they could themselves be lawyers, notaries, or just enterprising local people looking to supplement their income. Agents often liaised with the pension lawyer and could be instrumental in the early stages of a pension claim and in pushing a pension claim along in the process. They helped applicants reply to questions from the bureau. On the other hand, claims agents could also be a hindrance because they falsified claims and failed to get proper documentation through eyewitness visits and testimonies.

On April 26, Moore completed a "Claimant's Statement" questionnaire where Lucy declined to be present at the examination of witnesses or to have an attorney representation. It is hard to know if Lucy was simply confident in her application or could not muster the financial investment to afford legal representation. She was "quite poor" after all, and every visit to the notary or attorney came with a fee. In her declaration of expenses related to the case, she claims "only an occasional charge of 25 cents to a notary." Asked if she had any "complaint to make as to the conduct, manner, or fairness" of the examination, she simply answered, "None." As a Black woman with two years invested in the process, now was not the time to point out an unjust system. She signs the Claimant's Statement with an "X."

Lucy's deposition, also transcribed by George Moore, followed. She begins her statement by saying she is "51 or 52" years old; again, the uncertainty of her birth date was a small hint of her past enslavement secreted in these formal documents. Lucy's deposition serves as a summary of the facts of her service as nurse, with whom she served, where she traveled with the regiment, and the nature of her service. She references her husband and fellow veteran John Nichols. The final paragraph of her statement is the most direct declaration that she was both promised and deserving of pay. She states, "I never received a nickle [*sic*] for my services as nurse; Dr. Brucker told me I would be paid, and I worked on in the hope of getting pay after a while. I was not under Miss Dorothea L. Dix. I was never in any hospital, but that of the 23rd In. Vols., and was with them till I was relieved at Indianapolis."

Moore must have found her endearing and genuine because a certain affinity for her emerges in his formal special examination report. On April 26, 1894, Moore submitted his special examination report from New Albany to the Commissioner of Pensions. The report is slightly more narrative and perhaps even compassionate, evaluating Lucy's story as "plain and unvarnished." Moore writes that he explained to Lucy her rights and that she declined to be present at the examination of witnesses. Instead, Moore states that "claimant was satisfied with the evidence after I had taken it, and read it to her before taking her final statement." He reiterates that Lucy was "verbally employed" first as a laundress for the Indiana 23rd and then as a nurse. The witnesses who corroborated her testimonies "pay high tribute" to her "fidelity, industry, and . . . skill in her capacity as nurse."

Remarkably, Lucy's personal sentiment and humanity shine through in this brief report. The examiner indicates that there is no material evidence for Lucy's service but that she held in her dear possession a photograph, a "souvenir of her services." In it, she stands central among a group of veterans of the Indiana 23rd Regiment during a recent reunion. The surviving 1898 photograph perhaps hints at what the scene may have looked like, though the photograph is not only of the Indiana 23rd. However, this photograph was so important to Lucy that she declined to submit it as material evidence. Moore decided not to cross-examine Dr. Byrn because his testimony "could not make the case any stronger."

His report concludes with a strong and definite affirmation of Lucy's service, stating, "Claimant has no documentary evidence of her employment by anyone having authority of the War Department, but her claim is one of merit and should be allowed. The witnesses, so far as I could learn, are perfectly reliable in every way." Moore chose his words carefully with implicit codes meant to signal to the Pension Office his evaluation of Lucy's moral standing. Not only was there sufficient evidence of her service to warrant a pension, but Lucy was morally deserving, an upstanding citizen worthy of pension, even though moral standing was not a requirement of pension awards. He demonstrated his belief in her character and the character of her "reliable" witnesses. Given the implicit biases against the morality of African Americans, they shouldered a greater burden of proof for their worthiness. On May 1, 1894, Lucy's case, presumably with the report, was sent to the Board of Reviews as part of the special examination. Lucy resumed life as a domestic, undoubtedly anxiously awaiting the results of the deliberations.

Meanwhile, in two Board of Reviews documents, officials debated the legitimacy of Lucy's appointment as nurse based on the technicalities of 1860s policy, not on whether she served. The document opens with this plain and devastating statement: "The Army Regulations in 1862 did not authorize Regt Surgeons to employ colored females as cooks or nurses, therefore the testimony of Asst Surgeon Spencer Byron and Lorenzo D. Emory cannot be accepted to show that clmt did ~~not~~ serve as nurse during the period claimed."

This is the first piece of official government correspondence that clearly indicates the color of Lucy's skin and that race was the determining factor deciding her pension case. It is unclear if officials gleaned the information from Lucy's own declaration in 1894 or perhaps from the special examiner who had met her personally in New Albany. Regardless, Lucy had resolutely battled gender and class bias in a flawed government system, but now the color of her skin became an almost insurmountable obstacle. The appointment was invalid because thirty years prior, when Black women were still routinely enslaved, Lucy could not legally be hired to do the work of a white woman or man, which meant she could not be rewarded for that work even in the post–Civil War era. Even this injustice pales in comparison to the experiences of other Black nurses who were applying for pensions. Some were subjected to painful public testimonies about their history as slaves that had little meaningful impact on their pension requests. Having declined to be present at the examination of witnesses, she may have been spared the more gruesome public questioning.

The reviewer in Lucy's case left the door open, however, recommending Lucy's case for yet another special examination to determine "in what capacity and by what authority she was employed," as though that remained questionable. The chief of the Special Examinations Division does not deny in his reply of May that Lucy served diligently but questions whether she was officially "employed as authorized by the Army Regulations of 1863." Special examinations were assigned when an applicant had insufficient evidence or when the government suspected fraud, and they significantly delayed the process. Fraud cases took precedent, and other more routine cases would await processing longer. Black applicants were more likely to be put into special examination. In a sampling of soldier pension requests, about half of Black soldiers went through "special examination" in contrast to only about 26 percent of white soldiers.

The question of Lucy's pension request was complex on so many levels. The only officially sanctioned female nurses were under Dorothea Dix's purview, and almost all were white. Thus, while Lucy bore the responsibility for verifying her service, the Bureau of Pensions initiated a behind-the-scenes debate about the policies. Lucy had three strikes against her: she was female, Black, and employed by a regimental hospital. The ensuing dispute between the bureau and the surgeon general was about females nurses in the regimental hospitals. On May 28, 1894, the Bureau of Pensions returned the claim to the U.S. Army surgeon general, Dr. George Miller Sternberg. The inquiry is when General Order No. 31 of 1861 was changed to allow female nurses in regimental hospitals. General Order No. 31 of 1861 stipulated that "women nurses will not reside in the camps, nor accompany regiments on the march." The surgeon general replied days later, "Respectfully returned to the COMMISSIONER OF PENSIONS. The records of this office fail to show date of change of General Order No. 31, of 1861, or that the said order was ever changed so as to allow female nurses in regimental or Brigade Hospitals."

In what amounts to a tit-for-tat between the Bureau of Pensions and the U.S. Army surgeon general, the bureau asks the surgeon general to reconcile discrepancies, though it's unclear which discrepancies. The note continues, "It is proper to add that Par. 1293 of the Army Regulations of 1863 does not seem to provide for the appointment of female nurses in regimental or brigade hospitals." Surgeon General Sternberg replies, "This office fails to comprehend the request of the Pension Office," and, later, "The term 'nurses' does not necessarily mean female nurses"—on the contrary, the same paragraph of the Army Regulations of 1863 directs that the "cooks and nurses will be taken from the privates."

The debate at hand, whether female nurses could be appointed to a regimental hospital, hinges on the following paragraph of the Army Regulations of 1863.

1293. The senior medical officer will select the cooks, nurses, and matrons (and, at posts where there is no hospital steward appointed by the Secretary of War, a soldier to act as steward), with the approval of the commanding officer. Cooks and nurses will be taken from the privates, and will be exempt from other duty, but shall attend parades for muster and weekly inspections of other companies at the post, unless specially excused by the commanding officer.—*Revised United States Army Regulations: with an appendix containing the changes and laws affecting Army regulations and Articles of War to June 25, 1863.*

Clearly, in the case of Lucy's regiment and many others, the Army Regulations did not align with practice. Surgeons were supposed to choose their nurses from the invalid privates in the ranks. The Army Regulations also did not address the 1861 declaration by General Benjamin Butler that allowed for people who escaped slavery to enter into service and earn freedom and protection as contraband of war. It was common practice for women, including women who escaped from slavery, to enter into the regiments and hospitals first as laundresses and cooks. Less common but still widespread, these cooks and laundresses were either promoted to or assumed many of the duties of nurse. Despite the widespread practice, "contrabands" are mentioned only once in the Army Regulations of 1863—in a paragraph on abstracts of issues, or a listing of military issued supplies by rank. Army practice did not align with official army regulations, so Lucy's hope for a pension stagnates on this critical issue.

Between July 1894, the last noted date of rejection, and January 1896, there was little official action on Lucy's pension case. However, in that time, the Woman's Relief Corps (WRC) recognized that the Nurses Pension Act was both inefficient and too narrowly applied. In the Fourteenth National Convention of the WRC in 1896, Annie Wittenmyer reported that the interpretation of the law prevented regimental nurses from procuring a pension—Lucy was not alone. Wittenmyer was given permission by the organization to take the matter to a congressional committee to "obtain a more favorable interpretation of the law." Wittenmyer also reported that the process for procuring a pension was arduous. Only eighty-five cases were completed in the year, with 100 still pending. Most of those claims that were rejected were on the basis of a strictly interpreted law established more than thirty years prior. Each month and year

LUCY NICHOLS. 3

To the honorable the Senate and the House of Representatives of the United States of America in Congress assembled:

Your undersigned petitioners, who are exmembers of the Twenty-third Regiment Indiana Volunteer Infantry in the war of the rebellion, would respectfully represent that Lucy Nichols, formerly Lucy Higgs, a colored female hospital nurse in the regimental hospital of said regiment, having applied for pension under the act of 1892 granting pensions to nurses, etc., and said claim No. 1130541 having been rejected on the ground that the records fail to show that said claimant was employed as such nurse by proper authority for the period of six months;

Now, therefore, we, the undersigned exofficers and members of said regiment, having personal knowledge of the fact that said claimant was a true and faithful nurse in the hospital of said regiment from the summer of 1862 until the close of the war and did render great and valuable service to the sick and wounded of said regiment and who at all times constant and untiring in her labors as such nurse. And now that she is old and infirm and greatly in need of aid, therefore we pray your honorable bodies to pass a special act granting her a pension at the rate of $12 per month to support her in her declining years.

Alexander S. Banks, Company E, Twenty-third Indiana; David H. Johnson, Company I, Twenty-third Indiana; Levi H. Brown, Company D, Twenty-third Volunteers; J. S. Knowland, Company I, Twenty-third Indiana; James J. Cummins, Company D, Twenty-third Indiana; John H. Bane, Company I, Twenty-third Indiana Infantry; Geo. S. Kendall, Company G, Twenty-third Indiana Volunteers; Charles H. Kepley, Company C, Twenty-third Indiana Infantry; J. W. Portlock (his x mark), Company D, Twenty-third Indiana Infantry; Chas. Edwards, Company K, Twenty-third Indiana Infantry; James W. Ashby, Company C, Twenty-third Indiana Volunteers, Galena, Ind.; G. W. Owens, Company E, Twenty-third Indiana Volunteers, Orchard, Mo.; William Mix, Company E, Twenty-third Indiana Volunteers, New Albany, Ind.; Granville Holtzlaw, Company E, Twenty-third, New Albany; John Koch, Company C, Twenty-third, Celina, Ind.; Edward Harrison, Company G, Twenty-third, Marengo, Ind.; Thomas T. Rossor, Company F, Twenty-third Indiana; W. S. McClure, Company D; Cyrus B. Lewis, Company E, Twenty-third; Lafayette Frederick, Company K, Twenty-third Indiana Volunteers; H. C. Ferguson, major, Twenty-third Indiana; John Jackson, second lieutenant, Company C, Twenty-third Indiana; Peter L. McDaniel; Peter Pope, sergeant, Company A, Twenty-third Indiana; D. S. Jocelyn, private, F, Twenty-third Indiana; C. W. Woods, private, K, Twenty-third Indiana; John McClara, private, I, Twenty-third Indiana; Joseph H. Van Meter, private, I, Twenty-third Indiana; Benjamin B. John, sergeant, Company F, Twenty-third Indiana; J. W. Hammond, ex-captain, commanding Twenty-third Indiana Volunteers; Benjamin F. Current, Company D, Twenty-third Indiana Infantry; James A. Tyner, Company I, Twenty-third Indiana Infantry; William W. Daley, Company K, Twenty-third Indiana Infantry; Norman Cunningham, Company F; Benj. C. Smith, Company E, Twenty-third Indiana; Christian Hoss, Company G, Twenty-third Indiana; William Andrews; W. J. Cearns, Company F, Twenty-third Indiana; Dan (his x mark) Meisenbretter, Company D, Twenty-third Indiana Volunteers; John W. Edmondson, Company E, Twenty-third Indiana Volunteers; Thomas Clark, late captain Company E, Twenty-third Indiana Infantry Volunteers; Charles E. Villier, Company D, Twenty-third Regiment Indiana Infantry; John Sendlewiok, A, Twenty-third Indiana; S. J. McPheeters, surgeon, Twenty-third Indiana; Wm. R. Burton, Hastings, Nebr.; L. A. Hollis; A. S. Baner, late captain Company G, Twenty-third Indiana; John J. Hardin, late captain Company E, Twenty-third Regiment; John A. McWilliams, Company I, Twenty-third Indiana; R. A. Simpson, Company E, Twenty-third Indiana; William R. Sisco, Company E, Twenty-third Indiana; Frank Doutaz, Company K, Twenty-third Indiana; E. P. Bruner, Company K, Twenty-third Indiana; S. K. Hooper, adjutant, Twenty-third Indiana Volunteer Infantry; Roy Allen, Company E, Twenty-third Indiana Volunteers.

This is the letter that was sent to Congress, as documented in the *Congressional Record*, and signed by fifty-four veteran soldiers advocating on behalf of Lucy Higgs Nichols's pension application, 1893.

that passed for these ailing and aging former nurses was another month without the financial assistance they deserved and needed.

Wittenmyer's tireless lobbying on behalf of the regimental nurses never really led to a definitive resolution, at least not in the House. However, perhaps it paid off in individual cases or within the Pension Bureau because Lucy's case was once again sent by the House for review by the Committee on Invalid Pensions on January 8, 1896. The fate of House Resolution 3532 granting Lucy a pension is not recorded in the *Congressional Record*, but clearly it did not pass because the battle was still being fought a year and a half later.

On May 23, 1898, Robert W. Miers, a Democrat from Indiana who served on the Committee on Invalid Pensions, submitted a report to the House of Representatives. Perhaps Miers received pressure to reopen Lucy's case from his constituents and Indiana peers in the House, such as Representative William T. Zenor, who was from Corydon, Indiana, near New Albany, where Lucy resided. Representative Miers presented to the House a favorable recommendation to pass the bill, stating that Lucy's "service and employment is not denied, but her application was denied at the Bureau because she was not employed by the authority recognized by the War Department as having such power." Indeed, the question at hand was who really held the power: the War Department, the Pension Bureau, or the House. It certainly was not an old and ailing Lucy who, according to Miers's report, was "very poor" and "unable to earn her living" with "nobody to rely upon." The report from the Committee on Invalid Pensions was accompanied by a sworn testimony from Lucy dated November 16, 1895, subscribed by her consistent friend Benjamin Welker. Lucy's undoubtedly enormous frustration is confined to one loaded and tense phrase. Lucy "feels aggrieved at [the] rejection" because she had served and had been promised pay. She was unaware that the surgeon who appointed her had no authority to do so, and why should she suffer the consequences of complex and unclear internal military policies? She did not reveal all of those sentiments directly in her testimony, but they are undoubtedly contained in her simple statement of grievance.

The Honorable R. J. Tracewell sent a letter, also dated December 19, 1895, imploring the House to "do all you can for this old and invalid colored woman who so nobly stood by the boys of the Old Twenty-third Regiment." Those "boys" rallied around Lucy one more time demonstrating undeniable strength in numbers. A remarkable *fifty-four* veterans of the Indiana 23rd Volunteer Regiment signed a petition advocating for Lucy's pension. Their typed names and rank took an entire page of the reports of the 55th Congress. They included those loyal to Lucy's battle, such as Benjamin Welker and Lafayette Frederick, both of whom had been there on the first day Lucy submitted her request nearly six years prior. The list included men from across the city, state, and even nation, such as Shadrack K. Hooper, who lived in Denver, Colorado. It was as if

Lucy led a charge of fifty-four veterans, all there to fend off any doubt that she was worthy. The House passed the bill, and it went to Senate for approval.

The Senate report on December 8, 1898, was followed by an unceremonious approval of the Special Act; perhaps they were unaware of the long battle. After more than six years confronting the racial and gender biases of the policies of the pre–Civil War era, Lucy finally received her just reward. Lucy's Invalid Pension document is scrawled through with the words "Special Act," and she was "approved for allowance under 'Special Act' at the rate of $12 per month from December 20, 1898." The act, signed by the chief clerk of the Department of the Interior, is a stark document with a simple and straightforward typed paragraph. Handwritten across the front was "formerly Lucy Higgs." Unbeknownst to the officials who filed the paperwork, that small phrase conjures so many difficult and traumatic memories of enslavement, excruciating loss, and harrowing battles, all left behind by the tenacious nurse Nichols as she sought a future. Lucy's relentless fight for a pension reveals some of the fundamental paradoxes of being a former slave living in a post–Civil War America. Lucy occupied a space between freedom and enslavement. On the one hand, she had the means and the connections to put up the fight, but, on the other, she was constantly reminded of her station as former property of the Higgs family. Her service and character were questioned throughout the process. Her race was an implicit but pervasive barrier.

It is unknown exactly how Lucy received the news of her victory, but it is certain that the local representatives wanted to publicly proclaim their support of Lucy and enthusiasm for her triumph. According to the *New Albany Evening Tribune*, Congressman William Taylor Zenor, a southern Indiana native who was born near Corydon and studied law in New Albany, concluded his letter to Lucy with this moving acknowledgment of her service:

> Aunt Lucy, I congratulate you upon this good luck as well as act of justice for your patriotic service and devotion to your country and to the boys composing the Twenty-third of which you were a nurse, who have rewarded your devotion and kindness to them in their need, standing by

THE TENACIOUS NURSE NICHOLS

you in your old age and need. I trust you will accept this as an evidence of the fact that good deeds and kindnesses bestowed are not without their just recognition in this world.

He signed his letter, "Very truly your friend. W. T. Zenor." Lucy's successful bid for a pension made local and national news.

Lucy's pension award was apparently the subject of some gossip. An article in the *New Albany Daily Ledger* less than a year after the approval has the headline "Lucy Nichols: A Great Deal of Misinformation Being Published about Her and Her Pension." The article reiterates the strength of Lucy's character, her devotion to service, and the need for support. Perhaps there was some question about whether she was deserving or in need of the pension.

The *Denver Post* ran a dispatch about Lucy's pension. Major Shadrach K. Hooper, a veteran of the Indiana 23rd Regiment who had by that point moved to Denver as a general passenger agent of the Denver and Rio Grande Western Railroad, got wind of the article by telegram. He wrote an endearing recollection of her story, including some of the few details known about Lucy's service and life. His recollection concludes with this statement:

> One of the few remaining [veterans of the Indiana 23rd Regiment]— and she is over 66—she is just as devoted today as she was when she turned away from her child's grave and followed us into the very jaws of death thirty-five years ago. She is welcome in every house and at every fireside left to the 23rd Indiana as an honored friend and guest, and the prayer of us all is that the years may deal gently with the loving old woman!

The *New York Times* even ran the headline "A Female Civil War Veteran: 'Aunt Lucy' Nickols [*sic*] of Indiana to Have a Pension." The article may have been a bit exaggerated for dramatic effect, claiming Lucy actually took up arms to fight in the Civil War, but it is a laudatory proclamation of her victory. It even goes so far as to suggest that Lucy, though seventy years old (again inaccurate), was strong enough to attempt to enlist with the New Albany company in the 1898 Spanish-American

War. According to the article, she even wrote two letters to President McKinley on the subject. There is no evidence to corroborate the claims, but the same article was reprinted almost verbatim a year later in California. Lucy's story had taken on almost mythic proportions as news spread across the country of this brave and resilient woman's service and recognition.

7

A NOBLE ENDING

COMMEMORATING AND REMEMBERING

Two days after the bill awarding a $12 monthly pension to Lucy Higgs Nichols was signed by President McKinley, a "very pleasant incident occurred" at a Friday night Sanderson Post meeting on Christmas Eve, December 24, 1898. Lucy arrived with an "immense and elegant" cake as a Christmas present for the "old boys," and she was ushered in respectfully. According to the *New Albany Daily Ledger*, the cake was "fit for a king" and enjoyed by all who admired "Aunt Lucy." It was, undoubtedly, an occasion for great joy and celebration. Not only was it a holy day, but Lucy had, with the help of many in the room, overcome the odds. She navigated a history and legal system rife with prejudices to finally get the recognition she deserved, the validation of her service from the highest seat of the country she served. Lucy remained humble, and she never failed to show her gratitude toward the soldiers through caring for them. The paper reported that "every one who [knew] Aunt Lucy and her devoted three years of service with the Twenty-third Indiana Infantry in the Civil War, [was] glad that her patriotic labors [had] at last been recognized and rewarded."

Lucy's dedication to the soldiers and remembrance of service was a considerable presence in local, regional, and even national commemorations. She was always in attendance at local Sanderson Post Grand Army of the Republic (GAR) meetings and Memorial Day celebrations. She also regularly traveled to attend bigger state reunions of Civil War and Spanish-American War veterans. One of the two known photographic images (see photo on page 2) of Lucy Higgs Nichols is a captivating photograph dated 1898, shortly after she began receiving her pension. The elderly Lucy is the sole female and the only person of color. She stands stately in the middle of a large group of war veterans at a reunion of the GAR that she diligently attended every year. She wears an elegant gown with a full skirt.

By all accounts, she was the star of the show, garnering more attention than any other member. She caught the Southern Railroad to English, Indiana, to join the celebration. The veterans present include soldiers of the Spanish-American War and the Civil War. The setting is the old reunion grounds north of English. The identities of only a few soldiers in the photograph are known, including Lemuel Ford, Winfield Scott Sloan, Peter Gottfried, Henry McCowen, John Sloan, Sherman Spears, and Samuel Morgan. Gottfried instigated the annual GAR reunions in 1887.

According to oral history, Lucy cooked for the men at the yearly reunions, usually beans in a kettle over an open fire. While this probably brought back memories of her wartime service, the mood and atmosphere were much more buoyant and celebratory. Men stayed in tents, wagons, or the nearby Sulfur Hotel. They brought with them horses and drums and told many fireside stories to reminisce. Lucy was a devoted attendee of the state reunions or "encampments," which were held in different locations each year, including New Albany and Georgetown. National encampments of the GAR were held in nearby cities, such as Indianapolis, Cincinnati, and Louisville. Perhaps Lucy attended those as well, but there is no formal record yet known as proof.

In addition to the annual encampments, a news article of 1901 shows Lucy attended an annual district convention of the Woman's Relief Corps (WRC) in Jeffersonville, Indiana. The WRC was a critical proponent of the fight for nurses' pensions. The article, likely misprinted, states that Lucy was appointed secretary of the association, though Lucy could not read or write. She was, however, invited to speak at the event. She was so overcome with emotion recalling the gruesome events of war that she was unable to complete her speech. Maybe she was recalling the brutal slash and burn of Sherman's campaign, the times she pulled one of her wounded soldiers from the field only to accompany him during his last breaths, or the loss of her entire family, including her daughter Mona. Lucy's tragic sacrifices flooded her memories. Even Lucy, who was unimaginably strong and resolute, could not stifle the traumas of her past.

Slavery, emancipation, and African American wartime sacrifice were important components to the WRC's commemoration of the Union cause; however, racial equality and civil rights were not a prevailing concern. Given Lucy's service record and her connection to the nurses' pension initiative, it is not surprising she would be asked to speak. However, the WRC had a mixed record on their approach to membership of African American women. The WRC did succumb to pressures to segregate their members, at least in the South, where Black women in the WRC were crucial in promoting the Union cause during the Civil War. In northern states, the WRC did not allow for segregated corps. Despite their recognition of the service of Black women to support the cause, the white female leadership of the WRC had a spotty record in their advocacy and support of Black corps and leaders well into the early twentieth century. Lucy's experience speaking for the WRC was, in all likelihood, a positive one. Many of the women who attended the meeting were probably at the same Memorial Day services as Lucy each year, and she was familiar with them. All probably were familiar with her story and gave her a platform to share her experiences.

Lucy's loyal patriotism was not confined to the members of her community. In 1901, Lucy attended the second inauguration of President McKinley, with whom, it seems, she had built a rapport. Not only had he signed the special act of Congress that granted her pension, but she had written him multiple letters when she wished to join the Spanish-American War efforts. She went to Washington, D.C., for the inauguration—it was her first time in the city since 1865, when she attended the march of the Grand Review at the conclusion of the Civil War.

Soldiers and Sailors Monument dedication on May 15, 1902, in Indianapolis. Courtesy of the Indiana Historical Society.

Meanwhile, commemoration of the Civil War was happening across the country, very often celebrating the sectionalism that divided the country and contributed to discord. The major memorial in Indianapolis was and continues to be unique among them. The Soldiers and Sailors Monument was proposed initially by a group of veterans in the 1870s during a meeting at the printing shop of the *Greencastle Republican*. The editor, George J. Langsdale, proposed a downtown Indianapolis monument, and the GAR took the reins of the project before turning it over to the state. In 1887, the General Assembly appropriated $200,000 for the monument, and Langsdale was selected as president of the commission. The monument was dedicated in 1902, commemorating Hoosiers that served in the Revolutionary War, the War of 1812, the Mexican War, the Civil War, the wars of the frontier, and the Spanish-American War. Given Lucy's eager participation in patriotic and commemorative events and reunions across the state and nation, it is very likely she joined her fellow veterans from New Albany to attend the dedication. The monument is unique because it acknowledges not only the preservation of the Union and the sacrifices and heroism of soldiers but also the role of Union soldiers in the emancipation of enslaved people.

The monument has a substantial sculptural program, including two large sculpture groups on two of the four ends. They represent allegories of War and Peace. In the Peace grouping, Lady Liberty is the focal point of these large-scale, high-relief, in-the-round sculptures. Liberty charges forward bearing the flag. In her wake and in the register below, soldiers return home to greet their children, kiss their wives, and embrace their mothers as prodigal sons. Although hundreds of thousands of Black soldiers served in the commemorated wars, the only Black figure is a bare-chested man in torn pants lying on the ground. He props himself up on one hand while his leg and bare foot dangle over the ledge. He is lower than all of the other figures, almost powerless, and desperately lifts his gaze and his chains up to Lady Liberty. His shackles are broken as a symbol of his freedom. While including the image of the Black man was significantly better than the omission of emancipation outright, it is still a passive representation. Still, the memorial was unusual in its commemoration of emancipation. While the soldiers return to their families having completed their mission to preserve the Union, the Black man is just emerging from his shackles to seek out a potential future. Striking in its scale, the entire monument is only fifteen feet shorter than the statue of liberty. If Lucy and John were there to witness the dedication with thousands of others on May 15, 1902, it would have been a deeply moving experience as they reflected on their service and the life they built together after the Civil War. For illiterate former slaves who had served in the Civil War, visual commemoration such as monuments and Memorial Day celebrations were an important component of remembrance.

Around the same time the Soldiers and Sailors Monument was dedicated, New Albany's Carnegie Library in Lucy's hometown began construction. She probably passed by the construction site, watching the grand classically inspired building be erected. Dedicated in 1904, Lucy's access to the library would have been limited by segregation laws that demanded public facilities be separate but equal. Nor was she able to read. This library would eventually become the Carnegie Center for

Art and History, which housed a long-standing exhibition dedicated to remembering Lucy's life that opened in 2012.

RECOGNITION

News continued to spread far and wide of Lucy's triumph in receiving a pension through a special act of Congress—from St. Louis to Nebraska and beyond, she was recognized for her valor and service. Six years after Lucy's pension was awarded, her story continued to resonate. Occasioned by a stroke she suffered in August 1904, Lucy's journey, along with the only other known photographic image of Lucy, was printed in the *Indianapolis Freeman*. In this image, Lucy is shown with neatly coiffed hair and with a high-necked plaid gown with elegant details. She dons earrings and a broach at her neck. These small details of refinement are not merely fashionable but also symbols of her independent financial status and ability to acquire little luxuries. She could use her labor to acquire goods and purchase things that gave her pleasure, confidence, and status. The silk dress she wears stands in stark contrast to the simple cotton dresses she probably wore in her years of forced servitude. She exudes self-assured, hard-won dignity in the simple bust photographic portrait.

Launched in 1888 to a national audience, the *Freeman* was the first illustrated Black newspaper. The second paper launched by Edward E. Cooper, the newspaper declared that it was a "newspaper published, owned, edited and controlled by a Negro for Negroes" and that it would "bravely tell the Truth without fear or favor and is Fearless in the Advocacy of his Rights." The paper prided itself on highlighting the achievements of Black men and women. Newspapers for free Black people had been around since the Antebellum period. They covered a whole range of subject matter, not least of which was the abolition of slavery. What distinguished the *Freeman* was that it was the first illustrated Black newspaper, founded by Edward E. Cooper in 1888 and running through 1927. Cooper was a well-known if controversial figure in journalism. In the legacy of Antebellum Black papers that sought to have Black editors and readers who were not constrained by the white press, the *Freeman* enjoyed a large circulation because of its news coverage's variety and scope and its attention to Black culture. Subsidized by the Republican

One of only two known photographic images of Lucy Higgs Nichols, from the "Negress Who Nursed Soldiers Is a Member of the GAR," *Indianapolis Freeman*, September 3, 1904.

Masthead of the *Freeman*, the first illustrated Black newspaper that launched to a national audience in 1888. It was known for a commitment to art and highlighting Black achievement.

Party for some of its existence, the *Freeman* acquired a reputation as the country's leading Black journal in the 1890s.

The *Freeman* achieved this status with a team of correspondents covering issues and events of interest to African Americans across the nation. In 1889, Mississippi correspondents wrote of opportunities in the Yazoo Delta region and encouraged Blacks to migrate to Arkansas, Kansas, and Texas. The *Freeman* provided extensive coverage of the 1893 Cincinnati conference on Black progress and reported on discrimination and prejudice, such as the 1892 incident in Harrisburg, Pennsylvania, where painters went on strike because they did not want to work with a recently employed Black man. In 1897, the *Freeman* also reported on lynchings in the South, providing information on victims' race and other statistics starting from 1885.

The *Freeman* was known not only for its editorial content but also for its imagery that gave visual representation to Black culture in the late nineteenth century. Their aim was to represent "the colored race as it is, and not as it is misrepresented by many of [their] white contemporaries." A staff of artists created political and comic cartoons, some of which are controversial because they caricature Black Americans. They also created engravings to reproduce photographic images that had been produced elsewhere of prominent Black Americans such as Lucy. Shortly after the paper began, the *Freeman* began incorporating a front-page series of portraits representing upstanding Black citizens to encourage the visibility and recognition of respectable African American character. The portraiture series emphasized journalists, pastors, entrepreneurs, politicians, and other individuals who were involved in their local, regional, and national communities and civic engagement. These initiatives were part of a broader narrative of "racial uplift" propagated by Black elite intellectuals such as W. E. B. Du Bois, who wrote, "We want to be Americans, full-fledged Americans, with all the rights of American citizens." He envisioned the creation of an elite group of educated Black leaders, the "Talented Tenth," who would lead African Americans in securing equal rights and higher economic standards. In other words, racial advancement depended on the ability to witness contemporary Black achievements, challenges, and injustices to mobilize self-determination. As the *Harper's Weekly* of illustrated Black newspapers, Lucy's feature was a testament to the power of her story and preserves her rare remaining photographic likeness.

As remarkable as Lucy's story seems, she was not the only formerly enslaved female nurse of the Civil War. She joins a list of veritable heroes. Harriet Tubman, most well known for her efforts to aid fleeing freedom seekers on the Underground Railroad, was a nurse, cook, scout, and spy for the 1st South Carolina Volunteers Regiment. She also worked at the Freedmen's Hospital in Washington, D.C., and as a nurse and teacher in

Elizabeth Fairfax was a Black Civil War nurse who was a member of the GAR, shown here wearing a silk badge for the General N. B. Baker Post of the GAR, organized in Clinton, Iowa. Her cabinet card photograph is by William Frazer Ferguson. National Gallery of Art, Ross J. Kelbaugh Collection. Purchased with support from the Ford Foundation.

North Carolina. After the war, she was appointed matron for the Colored Hospital at Fortress Monroe, Virginia, and she established the Harriet Tubman Home for Aged and Indigent Negroes in 1908 in upstate New York. She applied for a nurses' pension but never received one despite advocacy on her behalf. Ultimately, the pension she received of between $8 and $20 per month was as a Civil War widow, not as a nurse. She was buried with military honors. Sojourner Truth, famed abolitionist and activist, also worked at the Freedmen's Hospital, the first hospital that offered medical care to freedmen. During Reconstruction, she advocated to provide better sanitary conditions as a nurse and counselor with the National Freedman's Relief Association.

Nor was Lucy the only Black woman to receive a pension. Susie King Taylor, Maria Bear Toliver, Elizabeth Fairfax, and Anne Stokes, among others, also received pensions for their work as nurses. Despite claims to the contrary in newspapers across the country, Lucy was not the only Black woman admitted to the GAR. There are remarkable correlations between the life of Elizabeth Fairfax and Lucy Nichols. Elizabeth Fairfax had escaped enslavement; served as a laundress, cook, and nurse in the Civil War; battled for a pension; and was honored with a GAR membership. She was even photographed wearing the GAR badge of Clinton, Iowa, in a formal cabinet card. She was lovingly referred to as "Aunt Liz" by her community. Like Lucy, she also attended many of the annual veteran encampments and Memorial Day processions in her Iowa town. She was honored with a veterans' burial in Clinton. There are undoubtedly others like Lucy and Elizabeth Fairfax whose stories are yet to be uncovered or connected.

ALWAYS A FIGHTER

While Lucy's harrowing story of service and victorious pension fight spread across the nation, Lucy was living a humble and quiet life on Naghel Street with her husband John, who was listed as the head of household in the 1900 census. He owned their home with a mortgage and was employed as a day laborer for most of the year. In this census, John Nichols is listed as having the ability to read and write. While still uncommon, it is possible that he received some sort of education as the child of free parents.

In the same year as Lucy's feature in the *Freeman*, the *Washington Times* printed an article stating she was critically ill with a "stroke of paralysis," and the soldiers came to her aid. By this point, Lucy was too weak to attend church regularly, but she always managed to go on Memorial Day Sunday services. John continued to work as a laborer, now at the Iron Mill.

Despite her ailments, Lucy always fought for her rights, and she never hesitated to use the power of the press to bolster her self-advocacy. In 1907, several news sources across the state proclaimed that Lucy "signified her desire" to be buried in the National Cemetery of New Albany. In that year, the superintendent of the National Cemetery, James Albertson, received orders that all army nurses who receive a pension or have certificates of service should be entitled to the privilege of burial in the cemetery. The same honor should have been afforded to Lucy's husband John as a veteran of the USCT. Perhaps together they imagined sharing the full honor of a rightful burial.

New Albany, Indiana, where Lucy and John resided, is home to one of fourteen original Civil War National Cemeteries. It was established in 1862 because New Albany was home to an important hospital center for the Union. One of the hospital's doctors designed the five-and-a-half-acre cemetery. In addition to serving as the burial ground for soldiers who died at the New Albany hospital, the more than 5,000 internments include veterans of the Civil War, the Indian Wars, the Spanish-American War, World Wars I and II, the Korean War, and the Vietnam War. This is the same cemetery that had been the site of some controversy in the early years postwar, when community members refused to commemorate Memorial Day because of the Black soldiers buried on a segregated plot on-site. Sadly, neither John nor Lucy is buried in the National Cemetery in New Albany or elsewhere, and there is no clear indication of what prevented them from receiving their honorable recognition.

By 1910, both John and Lucy were ailing from age. A census report from 1910 lists Lucy's name and the title of wife beneath her husband John Nichols, and they had been married for thirty-eight years by this point. His occupation was fireman for a rolling mill where iron was shaped by heat, but he had been out of work for twenty-six weeks of the year, and she had no occupation at all, likely a sign of decline in health for both.

On October 7, 1910, John drove Lucy in a carriage to the closing session of the annual reunion of the 23rd Regiment. On November 12, John Nichols died in his home at the age of seventy-two. For reasons unknown, he was not buried at the National Cemetery and is presumed to be buried at the historically Black cemetery in New Albany known as West Haven, though no tombstone marks his burial. According to his obituary, he was formerly a sexton of the "colored cemetery," though which cemetery is unclear, and he was a member of the United Brothers of Friendship.

The United Brothers of Friendship was originally a benevolent order for both freemen and enslaved members that was established in 1861 in Louisville, Kentucky. It formed just prior to the Civil War in meetings at private homes in Louisville and likely had a role in the Underground Railroad. When war broke out, they organized around the call to take up arms and maintained a weakened membership through the war. In a history of the organization published in 1897, the writer proclaims,

> While we have no discussion in our ranks about our legality as an order, from whom we abstained our charter, or of our right to assemble in State or National Grand bodies on account of our color, we affirm that none of these questions disturb us, for we have accepted the badge of distinction, and therefore are not elbowing our way into any white organization; we claim to be purely Negroes and of Negro origin.

The organization later became a "grand and secret order composed of male and female members" with more than 60,000 members in various states, Liberia, Canada, and the West Indies. This membership included females referred to as the Sisters of the Mysterious Ten. No evidence exists to suggest that Lucy was a member of the organization as well, but it is certainly a possibility that they shared this affiliation. The New Albany United Brethren of Friendship had been established by the early

1870s, the first National Convention was held in 1875, and, by 1877, they had organized one lodge and two temples in New Albany. It is tempting to see John's public affiliation with this organization as evidence of his own activism.

John's will, dated November 11, 1910, left everything to Lucy in the care of Reverend Manuel and his wife Cordelia, with the "express condition that Rev. Stolford C. Manuel and Cordelia, his wife, shall have cared for, provided for, and comfortably maintained my wife, Lucy, from the time of my decease until the death of my said wife . . . if they fail to do so, the will is null and void." The executor was Lafayette Frederick, the same man who served with her in the war and as witness in her depositions for a pension.

Probably unable to care for the home and her health alone, Lucy moved to 80 East 18th Street, the residence of Reverend Stolford C. Manuel, who was pastor of the Second Baptist Church from 1897 to 1910. Lucy was married to John for four decades. After his death, she was forced to move either by stipulations of the will or by limitations of her health and finances that were tied to Manuel. She left behind her beloved home, her garden, her furniture, and small trinkets and treasures, all the memories gathered over the course of nearly forty years in the home. Amidst the grief of losing her devoted husband, she had to leave the home they built together.

The arrangement, however, did not suit Lucy's fiercely independent nature. And Lucy had already learned she could navigate the legal system to maintain control of her destiny. Around March 1911, Lucy filed with the courts to reject provisions made for her in John's will and elected to take her statutory rights under the law. Via her lawyers Zenor and McIntyre, Lucy paid $1.50 to have the property of John Nichols appraised. The value came back at a value under $500. Lafayette Frederick, one of the men who had served as a witness on her pension applications decades earlier, was allowed a $10 administrator fee. The court ruled that "the whole of the estate of John N. is vested in Lucy Nichols, widow." Shortly after, Lucy moved back to her home on Naghel Street and resumed working as a laundress. She even filed an application to Congress in 1913 to increase her pension to $30. At each stage of her life, Lucy never

Civil War veteran and GAR member Edmund Caye was appointed Lucy's guardian in 1914. Detail from Sanderson GAR Post Memorial Picture, 1903. Courtesy of the Floyd County Library, New Albany, Indiana.

hesitated to take control of her own destiny. She was a spitfire who would not allow her race, age, or sex to deny her the freedoms and rewards for a lifetime of labor.

In 1912, a law had passed that increased the pension for Civil War veterans to $30 per month. For the past decade, pension laws were increasingly generous to veterans based on age and senility. There was a surprisingly wide range of pension amounts that varied according to age, health status, and law. For most pensioners already on the rosters during a 1907 update to the laws, they were automatically increased to new rates. It does not seem to be the case with Lucy because around 1913, Lucy apparently submitted an application to increase her pension, though the request does not appear in her official pension records. The only record of her request comes from a curious news article. In all likelihood, she enlisted the help of her influential veteran friends and acquaintances who were unhappy with the slow response to Lucy's request. It seems as though there had been some powerful advocacy on her behalf because the article in the *Louisville Courier* shows that the Honorable William E. Cox, state representative for New Albany's district, had received a letter inquiring about a pension increase request for a Mr. "Louis" Nichols, who did not appear on the pension rolls. Despite all of the success and national attention Lucy had received for being a Black woman on the pension rolls, there were still implicit biases that made the men in command assume that a pension request was obviously for a man. Even more intriguing was the newspaper covering the story, acknowledging the status that she continued to hold in the community well into her old age and disability. There is no record of her gradual increase in pension, although there should have been because pension records of Civil War soldiers should contain all requests for increases in pension. There is a letter, however, from 1914 indicating that her pension of $36 should be written to Edmund Caye, who had been appointed her guardian by the Circuit Court of New Albany. Lucy's self-advocacy and the support of those lifelong acquaintances continued to pay off.

Ailing Health

At seventy-two years old, Lucy's health had declined considerably. She could no longer care for herself. The Sanderson Post GAR members had done all they could. On January 5, 1915, Lucy was moved to the County Poor Asylum. Poor asylums, alternatively known as almshouses, poorhouses, infirmaries, and homes for the aged and infirm, were government- and charity-funded organizations that provided housing and care for "vulnerable" populations, such as the poor, elderly, and diseased. These institutions existed in America for hundreds of years, built by cities and counties, and were the foundation of other social services, such as nursing homes, mental asylums, schools for the "feebleminded," drug and alcohol treatment facilities, and homes for unwed mothers. In poor asylums across the country, these populations (and others) would live in the same place. Lucy was placed in the home in part because of her inability to earn an income, but also because of her age and debility. Lucy was among the "respectable aged poor" who needed medical care at the end of her life. Most of the people admitted to the almshouses were there voluntarily, but they were called "inmates." The term represented "almost every kind of human distress," according to Alexander Johnson in 1911, who wrote a book on the construction and management of almshouses. Almshouses provided for the care of the poor, the feebleminded, the chronically ill, the aged poor, the contagiously diseased, the deaf and blind, "tramps," and even, in certain cases, "delinquents" or criminals. In other words, an almshouse provided for a wide range of public dependents *and* public nuisances.

In Floyd County's asylum in 1910, there were only six "colored paupers" in the asylum amidst many white and native inmates. Conditions in asylums varied from institution to institution, but the Indiana Department of Public Welfare reported in 1920 that the Floyd County asylum's "inmates" seemed to be "properly taken care of and contented," and the asylum had addressed poor living conditions for colored inmates cited in a previous report. According to the Indiana State Statutes of 1899 Law Governing Asylums, every inmate was required to do a "reasonable amount of labor," though Lucy's age and debility would excuse her from the requirement. Because of the wide breadth of conditions in an almshouse, the classification of its residents was of utmost importance to provide for order and comfort, according to Johnson. Special care was bestowed on the old and infirm in the institutions, sparing them the more "unruly and vicious" of inmates. Lucy would have first been separated by her sex, including separate dormitories, recreation areas, and dining. This likely did not affect Lucy greatly, as she was at this point so ill that she was unable to participate in these daily routines. Poorhouses like the one where Lucy spent her last days were most common in the nineteenth and twentieth centuries, though their history goes back to the 1600s. The advent of Social Security effectively made problematic poorhouses obsolete, though the system was and continues to be an imperfect model for caring for the elderly and disabled.

On January 29, 1915, the *New Albany Daily Ledger* ran the headline "Only Woman Ever Member of the GAR Dies in Asylum: Was Noted Colored War Nurse." That morning, "Aunt Lucy" died in the County Poor Asylum after a long illness and paralysis. Lucy's funeral was at 1:00 p.m. the following day at the chapel of Newland Gwin's undertaking. The Sanderson Post GAR took charge of her funeral, and the expenses were covered by the city. The article in the *Ledger* closed with this moving tribute: "Aunt Lucy was known to almost everyone in this city and every one honored her for her loyalty."

She was buried with military honors beside her husband in the "colored cemetery." The location of Lucy's unmarked grave site is presumed to be in the historically Black cemetery West Haven, also known as West Union Cemetery and Rest Haven. Her home was near West Haven, and it is the most likely site of burial for a well-respected member of the Black community in New Albany. Other cemeteries for the Black community were family lots or for less affluent members of the community. One of the most notable is the "Colored People's Burial Ground," now dubbed Freedomland. The earliest known burials at Freedomland date from 1854, but the cemetery likely entered use earlier. Conservative estimates put the total number of burials around 300. The last internment is believed to have taken place in 1917. It is possible Lucy and John were buried there. Some Black citizens of New Albany were buried in the segregated plots in mostly white cemeteries near Fairview and the National Cemetery. The segregation of national cemeteries continued through 1948, when Harry S. Truman ordered the integration of the armed forces. Lucy, like John, is not buried in the National Cemetery despite being highly respected within their community and honored with GAR membership.

For her entire life, Lucy was dedicated to upholding the memories of her comrades and the fallen soldiers of the Civil War. She decorated their graves each Memorial Day, and she celebrated with the veterans at encampments and GAR meetings. Her loyalty to the troops and to her nation was unparalleled. Lucy was a fierce self-advocate, determined to receive the financial recognition she deserved for her years of service. The arc of her story—from young enslaved girl to doting mother, from freedom seeker to Civil War nurse, from grieving mother to loyal wife, from undocumented veteran to national celebrity—is nothing short of heroic. While her home and grave site have been lost to the ravages of time, her memory has been upheld by generations of storytellers, now preserved. Beloved "Aunt Lucy" and honored Nurse Nichols, may she rest peacefully in the dignity of an inspiring life well lived.

EPILOGUE

Storytelling is only one part of the process in writing a biography. There are hundreds of pages and hours of primary source research, or firsthand contemporary accounts of events, that provide the critical foundation and evidence for this book. Long before writing began, three historians local to New Albany, Indiana—Pamela Peters, historian and author; Curtis Peters, Professor Emeritus of Philosophy at Indiana University Southeast; and Victor Megenity, retired history teacher—conducted the bulk of the research. Without their diligent efforts, generous offer to share research, and kind collaboration, this book would not have been possible.

It was in 1995 that Pam Peters, author of *The Underground Railroad in Floyd County, Indiana*, conducted an oral history interview with Pearl Grundy Kimbrough, an elderly African American woman living in New Albany. At the time, Kimbrough's son lived in the home of Lucy and John Nichols on Naghel Street in the West Union neighborhood of New Albany. Kimbrough shared with Peters the story of Lucy. Through oral history, the story of Lucy's enslavement, escape, Civil War service, and settlement in New Albany had been preserved. The home, tragically, is no longer standing, demolished after 1996.

Lucy received mention in Peters's book on the Underground Railroad, but it was with the discovery of an 1898 photograph in the collection of the Indiana Room of the Floyd County Library that Peters initiated a decade-long quest to uncover and honor the story of Lucy's life. After many years of research, this is still only one of two known photographic images of Lucy Higgs Nichols. In it, she stands resolute and

Pearl Grundy Kimbrough tells historian Pamela Peters her family's oral history of the Underground Railroad, including the story of Lucy Higgs Nichols's home on Naghel Street in New Albany, Indiana, ca. 2000. Courtesy of Jennifer Suzanne Vezner.

dignified at the center of a reunion of Civil War and Spanish-American War veterans in English, Indiana, in 1898. The photograph is compelling.

Meanwhile, fellow local historian Victor Megenity ordered a copy of Lucy's pension records. Intrigued by the details present in these relics of Lucy's life, the Peterses and Megenity embarked on a multistate, years-long journey to uncover Lucy's story. They began in Bolivar, Tennessee, the city where Lucy met the Indiana 23rd Regiment and joined their ranks—first as contraband of war, then as laundress, and finally as nurse and comrade. They also went to Coffeeville, Mississippi, and the Peterses ventured to Halifax County, North Carolina, before returning to Bolivar. During these research trips, they found evidence of her childhood through extensive legal documents of the Higgs family: her enslavers. They also sought out the physical sites associated with Lucy's life, including an old log cabin on the property of Mary Higgs that could have been slave quarters. It was through travel to these critical sites of

Lucy's life that they could piece together her story through places and documents.

This research, coupled with Peters's research on the Underground Railroad, has provided the foundation for study of Black history in southern Indiana and the larger Ohio River valley region. The primary source research developed into a long-term exhibition at the Carnegie Center for Art and History in New Albany, organized by then director Sally Newkirk, a tireless advocate for Black history scholarship and understanding. Alongside an award-winning exhibition on the Underground Railroad, Lucy's story was brought to life for the general public. She became the subject of historical fiction books for adults and middle schoolers, historical reenactments, and public art.

As an art historian, I am particularly moved by the images that have been created to commemorate Lucy because art has the capacity to capture sentiments not easily expressed in historical narrative. The first was a bronze memorial portrait by David Ross Stevens; its clear intention was to capture a physical likeness of Lucy based on the scant photographic evidence. This sculpture resides in the collection of the Carnegie Center for Art and History. This artwork gives a tangible presence for Lucy, allowing her to take up space in the gallery that tells her story.

The second sculpture is an outdoor public artwork in the garden of the Town Clock Church (also known as the Second Baptist Church) in downtown New Albany, where Lucy's state historical marker is located. This is the same church where Lucy and John Nichols were members, and it is a documented site of the Underground Railroad. Over the past ten years, the church has been lovingly restored with the help of the Friends of the Town Clock Church, with leadership from Jerry Finn, Irv Stumler, Alice and Jerry Miles, and Reverends LeRoy and Joyce Marshall. This sculpture, unveiled on the fifty-fifth anniversary of the Civil Rights Act in 2019, is a life-size monument carved in high relief. The nine-foot-tall, ten-ton Indiana limestone sculpture by David Ruckman imagines Lucy's experience as she escaped from her enslavers. Her characteristic resolute expression appears here, too, looking into the distant future with determination and hope. She is shown carrying Mona, her young daughter, protectively in her arms across a stylized field of grass and trees. Lucy's

David Ross Stevens, *Lucy Higgs Nichols*, bronze. Courtesy of the Floyd County Library, New Albany, Indiana.

representation in the midst of self-emancipation has a deeply symbolic connection to the many people who crossed the Ohio River in search of safety and freedom in Indiana. Some used the tower of the Town Clock Church, situated on the banks of the river, to help direct them to the free shores of Indiana. The shared acts of resistance between Lucy and many other formerly enslaved people are symbolized by the site of the Town Clock Church and garden.

As of 2023, the newest addition to commemorative art in Lucy's honor is on the campus of Ivy Tech in Sellersburg, Indiana. The artwork was commissioned by Ivy Tech Community College as part of the second installment of the Soulful Nourishment Project, organized by Kofi Darku, commemorating the achievements of local Black heroes of the past through art. The marble sculpture by Louisville-based William M. Duffy was dedicated to Lucy Higgs Nichols to honor her important historical role in southern Indiana history and connection to the Underground Railroad while emphasizing the diversity of the campus and the grit that Lucy exhibited as inspiration for the student body. Duffy explains that the sculpture was meant to be not a portrait but instead a symbol of what Lucy stood for: strength, dignity, bravery, and honor.

Limestone sculpture by David Ruckman, unveiled in 2019 as part of the Underground Railroad Garden at the Town Clock Church (Second Baptist Church), New Albany, Indiana.

The abstract, bust-length human form emphasizes the heavy marble and the smooth finish. It is both strong and elegant, dignified and bold. For Duffy, commemorative sculptures acknowledging the contributions of Black Americans are necessary to counter the narrative told by Confederate monuments across the country, which he believes should be removed and rehoused for historical perspective.

In the Ohio River valley area surrounding New Albany, Indiana, there are many institutions that are committed to preserving and presenting Black history. The Carnegie Center for Art and History, now known as the Cultural Arts Center, has had long-standing exhibitions on the Underground Railroad and Lucy Higgs Nichols. The Frazier History Museum across the river in Louisville, Kentucky, has meaningfully expanded their exhibitions dedicated to Black history, particularly the Underground Railroad. Roots 101 African American Museum was established in Louisville in 2020. The institutions are too numerous to exhaustively detail. However, one organization is making strides in rediscovering and remembering the stories of enslaved people through the power of art. The (Un)Known Project creates artistic spaces and experiences to support learning, healing, reflection, reconciliation, and action by honoring the names and telling the stories of both known and unknown Black men, women, and children who were enslaved and hidden figures in Kentucky and beyond.

Although Lucy vocalized her desire to be buried in the National Cemetery, she does not have a gravestone there marking her burial. She is presumed to be buried at West Haven, the traditionally Black cemetery in her home's neighborhood of West Union. Community members are organizing in hopes to establish a gravestone in her honor there, and I hope to see her acknowledged with the military honors she rightfully deserves.

It is critical to document oral histories, invest in research and researchers, and preserve primary sources. Only through the process of rediscovery can we remember. Through writing, research, art, dialogue, and commemoration, remembrance paves a path toward a more just future.

William M. Duffy, *Stone Face*, bronze casting of marble original, 2021. Courtesy of Sherrolyn G. Duffy. In the collection of Ivy Tech Community College Sellersburg.

The Town Clock Church, also known as the Second Baptist Church, in New Albany, Indiana. Situated on the banks of the Ohio River, the church is a known site of the Underground Railroad. The church underwent significant restoration beginning in 2013.

ACKNOWLEDGMENTS

SEVERAL DEDICATED PEOPLE SERVED AS ADVANCED READERS OF THIS book, lovingly stewarding it to fruition at different stages. Among them are Pamela Peters and Sally Newkirk, both of whom are committed to seeing Lucy's story live on and were the most committed advisers; Jerry Finn, who is also a tireless volunteer working to preserve the Town Clock Church, where Lucy and John were members; Michael Jones, historian and author; and Kofi Darku, who calls "Aunt Lucy" one of the "Great Mothers" and a "Black Madonna." I also owe a debt of gratitude to the staff members who worked with me at the Carnegie Center for Art and History sharing Lucy's story to thousands of people over the years: Al Gorman, Daniel Pfalzfraf, Delesha Thomas, and Julie Liedner. Each of these people dedicated time, energy, and resources to this endeavor, compelled by Lucy's tragic but, most important, triumphant life.

SELECTED BIBLIOGRAPHY

"Appendix A: Union Army Pensions and Civil War Records." National Bureau of Economic Research. https://www.nber.org/system/files/chapters (accessed December 30, 2023).

Askeland, Lori. *Children and Youth in Adoption, Orphanages, and Foster Care: A Historical Handbook and Guide.* Westport, CT: Greenwood, 2005.

Baier, Marjorie, and Kiley Herndon. "What Price Glory: Dame, Bickerdyke, and the Fight for Pension Equity for Women." *American Journal of Nursing* 113, no. 10 (2013): 69–70.

Bentley, George R. *A History of the Freedmen's Bureau.* Philadelphia: University of Pennsylvania Press, 1955.

Berlin, Ira, ed. *Free at Last.* New York: Harcourt, Brace, 1992.

Blight, David W., and Jim Downs, eds. *Beyond Freedom: Disrupting the History of Emancipation.* Athens: University of Georgia Press, 2017.

Carpenter, Sue Pearson, and Margaret Lamb Atchley. *West Haven, an African-American Cemetery in New Albany, Floyd County, Indiana: Sometimes Recorded in Death Record as Rest Haven, West Street, West Union and Colored Cemetery.* New Albany: Southern Indiana Genealogical Society, 2004.

Casey, Jim. "'We Need a Press—A Press of Our Own': The Black Press beyond Abolition." *Civil War History* 68, no. 2 (2022): 1–15.

"Civil War Era National Cemeteries: Honoring Those Who Served: New Albany National Cemetery New Albany, Indiana." National Park Service. https://www.nps.gov/nr/travel/national_cemeteries/indiana/new_albany_national_cemetery.html (accessed December 29, 2023).

Clark, Robert L., Lee A. Craig, and Jack W. Wilson, eds. *A History of Public Sector Pension in the United States.* Philadelphia: University of Pennsylvania Press, 2003.

Coleman, Helen. *Civil War in Floyd County.* Undated (estimated late 1960s or early 1970s).

Collins, William J., and Robart A. Margo. "Race and Home Ownership from the Civil War to the Present." Bureau of Economic Research. http://www.nber.org/papers/w16665 (accessed December 29, 2023).

Cooper, Abigail. "'Away I Goin' to Find My Mamma': Self-Emancipation, Migration, and Kinship in Refugee Camps in the Civil War Era." *Journal of African American History* 2, no. 104 (Fall 2017): 444–67.

Davies, Wallace E. "The Problem of Race Segregation in the Grand Army of the Republic." *Journal of Southern History* 13, no. 3 (1947): 354–72.

Dowdy, G. Wayne. *A Brief History of Memphis.* Mount Pleasant, SC: Arcadia Publishing, 2011.

"Edward C. Cooper." Freeman Institute. https://www.blackhistorycollection.com/collection/edward-c-cooper (accessed December 29, 2023).

Etchison, Nicole. "The Legacy of the Civil War in Indiana." Indiana Historical Bureau. Accessed January 8, 2024, https://www.in.gov/history/about-indiana-history-and-trivia/annual-commemorations/civil-war-150th/hoosier-voices-now/the-legacy-of-the-civil-war-in-indiana (accessed January 8, 2024).

Gannon, Barbara. "'She Is a Member of the 23rd': Lucy Nichols and the Community of the Civil War Regiment." In *This Distracted and Anarchical People: New Answers for Old Questions about the Civil War–Era North,* edited by Andrew L. Slap and Michael Thomas Smith. New York: Fordham University Press, 2013.

———. *The Won Cause: Black and White Comradeship in the Grand Army of the Republic.* Chapel Hill: University of North Carolina Press, 2011.

Gibson, W. H. *History of the United Brothers of Friendship and Sisters of the Mysterious Ten: In Two Parts; a Negro Order; Organized August 1, 1861, in the City of Louisville, KY.* Louisville, KY: Bradley & Gilbert Company, 1897.

Gresham, Matilda, published under copyright of Otto Gresham. *The Life of Walter Quintin Gresham, 1832–1895.* Chicago: Rand McNally, 1919.

Hardeman County History Commission. *Hardeman County Historical Sketches.* Dallas: Taylor Publishing, 1977.

Harris, Duchess. *The Grand Contraband Camp.* Minneapolis: Abdo Press, 2019.

"Harrisburg Grand Review: November 14, 1865." African American Patriots of Pennsylvania. https://housedivided.dickinson.edu/sites/patriots/2010/07/22/harrisburg-grand-review-november-14-1865 (accessed January 1, 2023).

"Higgs, Lucy A., and John H. Nichols." Notable Kentucky African Americans Database. https://nkaa.uky.edu/nkaa/items/show/2435 (accessed December 31, 2023).

Holmberg, Jim. "'God Only Knows When It Will End': The Civil War Letters of Captain Benjamin F. Walter of the 23rd Indiana Volunteer Infantry Regiment." *Ohio Valley History* 11, no. 1 (Spring 2011): 69–77.

Hooper, Shadrach K. "A Historical Sketch of the 23rd Indiana Volunteer Infantry: July 29th, 1861, to July 23rd, 1865." Indiana-Vicksburg Military Park Commission, 1910.

———. "Twenty-Third Regiment Indiana Infantry Volunteer." In *Indiana at Vicksburg,* edited by Henry C. Adams. Indianapolis: Wm. B. Murford, 1911.

Hoskins, Jim. *Black, Blue, and Gray: African Americans in the Civil War.* New York: Simon and Schuster, 1998.

Hunter, Tera. *Bound in Wedlock: Slave and Free Black Marriage in the Nineteenth Century.* New York: Norton, 2021. Originally printed in 2017.

Indiana Battle Flag Commission, Mindwell Crampton Wilson, and David Isaac McCormick. *Indiana Battle Flags and a Record of Indiana Organizations in the Mexican, Civil and Spanish-American Wars*. Indianapolis: Indiana Battle Flag Commission, 1929.

Jenkins, Earnestine Lovelle. *Race, Representation, and Photography in 19th Century Memphis: From Slavery to Jim Crow*. London: Routledge, 2017.

Johnson, Alexander. *The Almshouse, Construction and Management*. New York: Charities Publication Committee, 1911.

Jones-Rogers, Stephanie. *They Were Her Property: White Women as Slave Owners in the American South*. New Haven, CT: Yale University Press, 2019.

Kay, Marvin L. Michael, and Lorin Lee Cary. *Slavery in North Carolina: 1748–1775*. Chapel Hill: University of North Carolina Press, 1999.

Kelbaugh, Ross J. "A Forgotten 'Veteran' Remembered." *Military Images Digital*. https://www.militaryimagesmagazine-digital.com/2022/11/13/a-forgotten-veteran-remembered (accessed November 22, 2023).

Kennedy, John C. "A Perfect Union: The Woman's Relief Corps and Women's Organizational Activism, 1861–1930." PhD diss., Purdue University, 2017.

———. "Race, Civil War Memory, and Sisterhood in the Woman's Relief Corps." Paper presented at the Proceedings of the Third Conference on Veterans in Society, Roanoke, VA, November 12–14, 2015.

King, Wilma. *Stolen Childhood: Slave Youth in Nineteenth-Century America*. 2nd ed. Bloomington: Indiana University Press, 2011.

LaRoche, Cheryl Janifer, and Patsy Fletcher. *Thematic Framework for the History of Civil Rights in the National Capital Area*. Washington, DC: National Park Service, 2021.

Lawson, Melinda. *Patriot Fires: Forging a New American Nationalism in the Civil War North*. Lawrence: University Press of Kansas, 2002.

Logan, Mrs. John A. *The Part Taken by Women in American History*. Wilmington, DE: Perry Nall Publishing Company, 1912.

Loperfido, Christopher. *Death, Disease, and Life at War: The Civil War Letters of Surgeon James D. Benton, 111th and 98th New York Infantry Regiments, 1862–1865*. El Dorado Hills, CA: Savas Beatie Publishing, 2018.

Masur, Kate. *Until Justice Be Done: America's First Civil Rights Movement, from the Revolution to Reconstruction*. New York: Norton, 2021.

Mays, Dorothy. *Women in Early America: Struggle, Survival, and Freedom in a New World*. New York: Bloomsbury Academic, 2005.

McConnell, Stuart. *Glorious Contentment: The Grand Army of the Republic, 1865–1900*. Chapel Hill: University of North Carolina Press, 1992.

Peters, Curtis H. "An 1862 Slave Escape and Its Lasting Impact: The 23rd Indiana Volunteer Regiment and Lucy Higgs Nichols." Unpublished essay, 2010.

Peters, Pamela R. Oral history interview with Crawford County historian Richard Eastridge, 2004. He received the information from Sherman Spears's son, his grandfather.

———. *The Underground Railroad in Floyd County, Indiana*. Jefferson, NC: McFarland, 2001.

Peters, Pamela R., Curtis H. Peters, and Victor C. Megenity. "Lucy Higgs Nichols: From Slave to Civil War Nurse of the Twenty-Third Indiana Regiment." *Traces of Indiana and Midwestern History* 22, no. 1 (2010): 34–39.

Ratzlaff, Aleed J. "Illustrated African American Journalism: Political Cartooning in the Indianapolis Freeman." In *Seeking a Voice: Images of Race and Gender in the 19th Century Press*, edited by David B. Sachsman, S. Kittrell Rushing, and Roy Morris. West Lafayette, IN: Purdue University Press, 2009.

Regosin, Elizabeth. *Freedom's Promise: Ex-Slave Families and Citizenship in the Age of Emancipation*. Charlottesville: University of Virginia Press, 2002.

Robinson, Kyle Brent. "Seeking a Hoosier Home: Black Migration to Indiana and the Politics of Belonging." *Concept* 34 (2011).

Rogers, Carol O. "Black and White in Indiana." *Indiana Business Review* 80, no. 2 (2005): 1–3.

Ryne, J. Michael. "'The Negroes Are No Longer Slaves': Free Black Families, Free Labor, and Racial Violence in Post-Emancipation Kentucky." In *After Slavery: Race, Labor, and Citizenship in the Reconstruction South*, edited by Bruce E. Baker and Brian Kelly. Gainesville: University Press of Florida, 2013.

Salmon, Marylynn. *Women and the Law of Property in Early America*. Chapel Hill: University of North Carolina Press, 1986.

Schultz, Jane. "Race, Gender, and Bureaucracy: Civil War Army Nurses and the Pension Bureau." *Journal of Women's History* 6, no. 2 (1994): 45–69.

———. *Women at the Front: Hospital Workers in Civil War America*. Chapel Hill: University of North Carolina Press, 2004.

Schwartz, Marie Jenkins. *Birthing a Slave: Motherhood and Medicine in the Antebellum South*. Cambridge, MA: Harvard University Press, 2006.

Shaffer, Donald R. *After the Glory: The Struggles of Black Civil War Veterans*. Lawrence: University Press of Kansas, 2004.

Slap, Andrew L., and Michael Thomas Smith, eds. *This Distracted and Anarchical People: New Answers for Old Questions about the Civil War-Era North*. New York: Fordham University Press, 2013.

Stauble, Mary Bayer. "Lucy Nichols." *Southern Indiana Genealogical Society Quarterly* 21, no. 1 (2000): 39–43.

———. "Lucy Nichols: Questions, Some Answers and More Questions." *Southern Indiana Genealogical Society Quarterly* 21, no. 2 (2000): 85–88.

Straubing, Harold Elk. *In Hospital and Camp: The Civil War through the Eyes of Its Doctors and Nurses*. Harrisburg, PA: Stackpole Books, 1993.

Taylor, Amy Murrell. *Embattled Freedom: Journeys through the Civil War's Slave Refugee Camps*. Chapel Hill: University of North Carolina Press, 2018.

Wagner, David. *The Poorhouse: America's Forgotten Institution*. Sheridan, WY: Gotham Books, 2021.

Wardrop, Daneen. *Civil War Nurse Narratives, 1863–1870*. Iowa City: University of Iowa Press, 2015.

Williams, Andrea N. "Cultivating Black Visuality: The Controversy over Cartoons in the Indianapolis 'Freeman.'" *American Periodicals* 25, no. 2 (2015): 124–38.

Woodworth, Steven E., and Charles D. Grear. *Vicksburg Besieged*. Carbondale: Southern Illinois University Press, 2020.

SELECT NEWSPAPER ARTICLES

Arcata Union (Arcata, CA), January 21, 1899.

"Aunt Lucy Nichols: History of a Distinguished Colored Woman." *New Albany Evening Tribune*, February 4, 1889.

"The Campfire at the Opera House Is a Grand Success." *New Albany Evening Tribune*, September 22, 1894, 4.

"Colored Mammy of Regiment Asking for Pension in Her Old Age. Nursed the Sick." *English Crawford County Democrat*, August 21, 1913.

"Congressman Zenor Notifies 'Aunt' Lucy of Her Good Luck." *New Albany Weekly Tribune*, December 16 1898.

Courier-Journal (Louisville, KY), July 29, 1884; September 14, 1884.

Daily Argus News. March 11, 1889.

"Daughter of the Regiment: An Indiana Negress with a Remarkable War History." *Janesville Daily Gazette*, March 14, 1889.

"Decorating the Graves: Memorial Services at the National Soldiers's Cemetery." *New Albany Evening Tribune*, May 30, 1892, 3, 4.

"Departure of the 23rd Regiment." *New Albany Daily Ledger*, August 15, 1861.

"District WRC Adjourns Its Convention at Jeffersonville." *New Albany Weekly Tribune*, October 18, 1901.

"A Female Civil War Veteran: 'Aunt Lucy' Nickols of Indiana to Have a Pension." *New York Times*, December 26, 1898, 1.

Fort Wayne Weekly Sentinel, March 10, 1875.

Freeman, December 16, 1899; August 24, 1907.

Liberator, June 26, 1863.

"Lucy Nichols. A Great Deal of Misinformation Being Published about Her and Her Pension." *New Albany Daily Ledger*, July 14, 1898.

"Name Confused: Aged Negro Woman's Pension Delayed." *Courier-Journal*, July 20, 1913, 28.

"Negress Who Nursed Soldiers Is a Member of the GAR." *Freeman*, September 3, 1904.

New Albany Daily Ledger, June 8, 1865; June 18, 1862; August 4, 1862; April 4, 1870, 2; July 23, 1884; September 13, 1884; December 13, 1898.

New Albany Evening Tribune, December 12, 1883, 3.

New Albany Weekly Tribune, March 8, 1901, 5; July 19, 1907; November 18, 1910, 4.

"Only Woman Ever Member of the GAR Dies in Asylum: Was Noted Colored War Nurse." *New Albany Daily Ledger*, January 29, 1915.

"Presentation." *New Albany Weekly Tribune*, December 31, 1897, 7.

Republican Indianapolis Journal, June 25, 1869.

"The Reunion." *Salem Republican Leader*, October 19, 1899.

"Sanderson Post-Aunt Lucy Nichols Gives the Veterans a Large Christmas Cake, Which They Enjoy." *New Albany Daily Ledger*, December 24, 1898.

"She Receives Her Pension." *Lexington Herald-Leader*, December 27, 1898, 4.

"The Veterans." *New Albany Daily Ledger*, August 25, 1886.

"Why Aunt Lucy Got a Pension—Major Hooper Tells Why, and after You Read the Major Story, You, Too, Will Say That Aunt Lucy Deserves That Pension." *Denver Post*, December 18, 1898.

DOCUMENTS

Bulletin. U.S. Government Printing Office. Vols. 111–112 (1914), 15.

Caron's Directory for the City of New Albany, 1880–1881.

Caron's Directory of the City of New Albany, 1888–1889.

The Civil War Archive—Indiana Units.

Combined Military Service Records for Calvin Higgs, National Archives.

Congressional Record: Containing the Proceedings and Debates of the Fifty-Second Congress. March 17, 1882, p. 1990; *Army and Navy Journal*, 1882.

Congressional Record: Containing the Proceedings and Debates of the Fifty-Second Congress. First Session, Volume XXIII, 1892.

55th Congress, 2nd Session, H.R. Report No. 4741 (to accompany HR 1366), June 23, 1898.

Floyd County, Indiana, Deed Records, Book 19, 30.

Floyd County, Indiana, General Affidavit for Claim No. 1130541, 29/07/1993.

Floyd County, Indiana, Grantor Book 19, January 7, 1871.

Floyd County, Indiana, Index to Marriage Record 1845–1920, Inclusive Volume, WPA Book Number Indicates Location of Record, Book 6, 572.

Floyd County, Indiana, Pension Office, Deposition #6, Case of Lucy Nichols, No. 1130541, April 12, 1894.

Floyd County, Indiana, Poor Farm Register. Floyd County Commissioners, 1915.

Floyd County, Indiana, Wills, Book 6, 224.

Halifax County Deed Books, Bk. 22, 225, No. 24, 225.

Hardeman County, Tennessee Records, Index to Marriage Record, January 1866.

Hardeman County, Tennessee Records, Inventory of Reuben Higgs' Slave Property, March 2, 1846.

Hardeman County, Tennessee Records, Inventory of Reuben Higgs' Slave Property, July 9, 1855.

Hardeman County, Tennessee, Petition of Heirs of John Higgs, 1855.

Indiana Archives and Records Administration; Indianapolis; Death Certificates, 1910, Roll 04.

John Nichols Will. Floyd County Circuit Court, Book G, November 11, 1910, 224–26.

Marriage license of John Nichols and Lucy Higgs, issued by Floyd County Circuit Court April 2, 1870. Certificate of marriage dated April 13, 1870, and signed by the Reverence. Marriage license dated December 14, 1893, in the records of the Pension Office.

National Archives at Washington, DC; Compiled Military Service Records of Volunteer Union Soldiers Who Served with the United States Colored Troops: Artillery Organizations; Microfilm Serial: M1818; Microfilm Roll: 89.

National Archives, U.S. Colored Troops Military Service Records, film 3M589.

New Albany City Directories.

Pension Records Lucy Higgs Nichols.

Public Welfare in Indiana. Department of Public Welfare. Issues 122–130 (1920–1921).

United States Congressional Senate Committee on Pensions, Congressional Serial Set Issue 3627, 1898.

United States Federal Census Records, 1830, 1840, 1850, 1860, 1870, 1880, 1890, 1900, 1910.

MANUSCRIPT COLLECTIONS

Clara Barton Papers, Library of Congress.

Letter from Colonel William L. Sanderson to his daughter, August 11, 1862.

Letter from Magnus Brucker to his wife Elizabeth, from Atlanta, Georgia, September 18, 1864. Indiana Historical Society, Magnus Brucker Paper, #M 0324.

Letter from Magnus Brucker to his wife Elizabeth, from Bolivar, Tennessee, March 8, 1862, Magnus Brucker Papers 1828–1874, Indiana Historical Society.

Official Records of the Union and Confederate Armies, vol. 10, series 1, 197. From the report of Colonel William L. Sanderson, March 10, 1862. In the collection of the Indiana Historical Society.

Petition from the Woman's Relief Corps requesting a pension, National Archives. https://catalog.archives.gov/id/306651.

Proceedings of the National Convention, Woman's Relief Corps, 1885.

Report of B. F. Potts, Col. 32nd Ohio Volunteers Commanding 1st Brigade, 4th Division, 17th A.C. Near Atlanta, Georgia, September 10, 1864. Indiana Historical Society Magnus Brucker Papers.

Report from the Committee on Pensions February 19, 1890, letter to Kate B. Sherwood from Annie Wittenmyer, submitted to the Senate by Sherwood.

Revised United States Army Regulations, with an appendix containing the changes and laws affecting Army regulations and Articles of War to June 25, 1863. https://collections.nlm.nih.gov/catalog/nlm:nlmuid-101556516-bk.

Sixth National Convention, Woman's Relief Corps, September 13, 1888, 27.

William T. Sherman, Special Field Orders No. 120, November 9, 1864, *Civil War Era NC,* https://cwnc.omeka.chass.ncsu.edu/items/show/145 (accessed December 28, 2023).